Exploring Education

Childhood

A Sociological Perspective

M. D. Shipman

Senior Lecturer in Education
University of Keele

NFER Publishing Company Ltd.

Published by the NFER Publishing Co.,
Book Division, 2, Jennings Buildings,
Thames Avenue, Windsor, Berks, SL4 1QS

Registered office; The Mere, Upton Park, Slough, Bucks, SL1 2DQ

First Published 1972

© M. D. Shipman, 1972

85633 006 X

Printed in Great Britain by
John Gardner (Printers) Limited, Hawthorne Road, Bootle, Lancs, L20 6JX

Contents

Changes in the context of child rearing

THIS BOOK is concerned with socialization, the process of learning the behaviour patterns that enable people to interact meaningfully. Any study of the socialization of the young must start with a recognition of the great differences that exist between societies and within them. This book starts by drawing on evidence from societies at different times and in different places. It ends by comparing the evidence on different patterns of socialization within contemporary Britain.

The evidence from history and anthropology does more than illustrate variations in patterns of socialization. It provides the context within which evidence from the social sciences can be understood. The socialization of the young is organized by adults in order that successive generations shall learn the blueprint for living that we call culture. It will be argued throughout this book that this is not a straitjacket. The learner, even when very young, interacts, interprets and plays off one influence against others, thus exercising some control over what is learned. But socialization is a means to ends, and these ends, however diverse, are defined by adults to ensure that children grow up with the ability to communicate, to play their parts in adult society and to play them in ways that are approved. This approval of certain values, certain versions of good and bad, may not be universal. Coercion and indoctrination abound. But socialization is always a means to ends that some group accepts as proper or has had imposed on them.

The nature of children
At a time when the Devil, Hell, everlasting damnation and even Sin have disappeared from advice to parents and teachers it may seem anomalous to discuss the angelic or diabolical nature of childhood. We no longer worry about the likelihood of the early death of our children and are little concerned about their state of grace. High

infant mortality and the prevalence of disease lie behind the historical and anthropological evidence that follows.

The Christian concern with the salvation of children was an important influence over child-rearing and schooling until this century. But within this concern were two contrasting views of the nature of children, fluctuating in emphasis, but detectable at all times. One view stressed the angelic, unsullied, natural goodness of children. The other stressed their devilish, potentially evil, self-willed nature. These perspectives required very different methods of child-rearing and training if the objective of an adult capable of distinguishing good and evil was to be accomplished. Similarly Ariès (1962) distinguishes a 'coddling' attitude towards children from another tradition stressing the need for strict, detached moral guidance.

Ariès had argued that there was no concept of childhood in medieval Europe. The artist portrayed the child as a young adult. The infant was too likely to die, even in the wealthy families that could have portraits painted, to be of central importance. As soon as the child could live without the constant attention of the mother or nurse he joined adult society. The French had no word for the child in the first months of life until they borrowed 'baby' from the English in the Nineteenth Century. This was not a callous attitude, but a reflection of the continual presence of death and the importance of the family rather than the individual.

From the Sixteenth Century on there was a growing awareness of the particular nature of children. They were to become a major area of study. Manuals of advice to parents were to become plentiful. But the two views of children persisted from the Sixteenth Century to the present. At all periods writers can be found expressing their faith in children as angels or their fear of them as possessed of natural sin.

The harsh view of children saw them as foolish and stubborn, and this spirit had to be broken for their ultimate good. The strength of Puritanism in the Seventeenth Century reinforced this view. The importance of individual salvation gave moral sanction to the use of the rod in family and school. The flavour can be gauged from the following passages from Puritan writers and preachers quoted from Pinchbeck and Hewitt (1969). 'O Hell is a terrible place, that's worse than a thousand whippings; God's anger is worse than your Father's anger.' 'The devil rocks the cradle.' 'Be much . . . . in the contemplation of the four last thyngs, Heaven, Hell, Death and Judgement. Place yourselves frequently on your death beds, in your Coffins, and in your Graves.'

This harsh attitude persisted into the Nineteenth Century. The Evangelicals saw child-rearing as a battle against depravity, original sin that had to be won with firmness and method. Sangster (1963) points out that only the Evangelicals deliberately used the fear of death as an instrument of education and considered it a necessary step to conversion. At a time when three children out of four would die before the age of five years it was relevant for children to sing:

There is an hour when I must die,
Nor do I know how soon 'twill come:
A thousand children, young as I,
Are called by death to hear their doom.
(I. Watts, Hymns, *Solemn Thoughts of God and Death*.)

Alongside this Puritan, Evangelical tradition of harshness, lay another view of children. This was to flower in the 'cult of childhood' (Boas, 1966). Here the child was seen as the innocent, the ideal man, the pure in heart. This perspective lies parallel to the more morbid view. It was present when Puritanism was strong. Earle (1628) wrote that the child '. . . . is the best copy of Adam before he tasted of Eve or the apple; and he is happy whose small practice in the world can only write his Character. He is Nature's fresh picture newly drawn in oil, which time, and much handling, dims and defaces. His soul is yet a white paper unscribbled with observations of the world, wherewith, at length, it becomes a blurred notebook.' This is very close to the view later taken by Rousseau and other forerunners of modern educational practice.

As the Evangelicals were shaping English education and family life in the early Nineteenth Century on the basis of the devil in the child, Blake and Wordsworth were expressing the innocence of childhood (Coveney, 1957). But this was not just a conflict of view on the nature of children. Rousseau particularly was saying something entirely new in his *Emile*. The child is not a man but a creature in his own right, requiring special consideration. This combination of romanticism, compassion and a focus on childhood as a special period, not just the start of adulthood, is the basis from which the evidence on socialization in our 'century of the child' must be viewed.

There is however one thread continuing through these contrasting views on children, and indeed through all the evidence on socialization from history and anthropology. Despite the variety of beliefs and practices in socialization that makes the normal of one society the abnormal in another, there is a universal concern with the morality of the young, whether this is to be secured through beating out the evil in them or fostering the good. This is easier to see in simple, pre-literate societies where children are taught to identify fully with the tribe. The first concern of parents and kin here is to ensure that children grow up in the parental ways.

Startling contrasts should not obscure this emphasis on promoting identity. The apparent sexual freedom of children under the palms of Samoa as described by Mead (1943) should not be taken as an abdication of parental authority. Indeed, in many pre-literate societies the whole tribe take responsibility for each child. It is a genuinely educative community. Punishment for wrongdoing may not be severe, but moral guidance is universal. It can be best understood from authors writing from their own indigenous knowledge such as Kenyatta (1953), Moumouni (1968) or Ammar (1954).

This is moral education in the full sense. It is usually planned and systematic. Once the scale of a society starts to increase or it starts to organize for warfare, the elements of schooling can be detected. This often takes the form of the segregation of groups of children of the same age for instruction. Many African Kingdoms organized 'Bush' schools, rather like our own public schools, in which boys were sent into the jungle under older, learned men, to learn the ways of the tribe. Although this training included preparation for fighting and for occupation, it mainly concentrated on the religious and moral life of the tribe. What was not left to chance was the personality of the child. The dependence of small scale societies on the identity of the individual within the group accounts for the frequency with which initiation rites have been found to mark the transition from childhood to adult status. These rites could be very long and complicated or short and simple. At their most sophisticated they were similar to the education of the young in the ancient Greek city states. There was a clear and often painful division between the child and the adult. While mainly confined to boys, there was often a shorter preparation of girls for marriage. For both boys and girls, there was often mutilation of the body to mark the transition. For boys this was often a severe test of physical endurance. Individual physical courage was necessary to social survival. It too could not be left to chance.

The concern for maintaining social order through the socialization of the young in family and school persists (Shipman, 1971). All peoples, regardless of religious or political beliefs are concerned with the behaviour of children because they are the next generation. This concern may be expressed in profound religious doctrine and ritual. It may be only a desire by parents and teachers for a quiet life. But in all societies, at all times, the learning of the young is organized to promote a particular type of identity, the ability to communicate and some respect for adult authority. There may be great variations in interpretation and implementation within each group, but socialization is never left to chance. Social life is organized on the basis of constraint over the young.

The universality of socialization nevertheless includes very different patterns. Bronfenbrenner (1972) suggests that the English pattern is nearest to the American in the independence of children and parents. In the USSR children and adults remain in closer contact. Indeed Bronfenbrenner sums up the new American pattern of child-rearing by saying 'children used to be brought up by their parents.' American and English children are seen as more willing to be anti-social than those in Russia or the other countries studied. Teachers, and others in authority in countries with Anglo-Saxon traditions, may have a hard time. They are also less liable to be supported by the intervention of parents, particularly fathers, in the lives of the children. A comparison of Scottish, American and Russian children by Paton and Beloff (1970) using Bronfenbrenner's ideas came to similar conclusions. In Russia parents, teachers and peers seem to reinforce each other's influence. In Britain and the USA the teacher may be opposed by these other influences.

The limits of childhood
The little account that was paid to childhood in medieval Europe meant that it was natural to treat children as adults, however miniature, at an age when our children would just be entering infant schools. This involved playing a part in adult working and social life often under an harsh discipline to ensure that routines were quickly learned. Apprenticeship started at around seven years, and among the more wealthy, children were sent into other households to learn manners, to serve and to master a trade.

In a period when there was no tailor-made world for the child, no special books, few schools, no legal limits on ages of entering work or school, childhood was not only short but lacked distinctive stages. Age meant less than it does today. Boys could go to university at 13. Marriage was often arranged at 14. There was no statutory definition of the ages for schooling or work to begin. Only with the 1563 Statute of Artificers was a seven-year period stipulated for apprenticeship. Only in 1833 was there an effective Factory Act keeping children under nine out of work. Only in 1889 were children recognized as having rights in law.

The situation was changed, not only through the extension of childhood, but in the recognition of distinct stages. Education was made compulsory for all children under ten in 1876 and children now stay until 16 years. The Education Acts specify three distinct stages of schooling, primary, secondary and further or higher. The primary schools are divided into infants and juniors. The Children and Young Persons Act of 1933 defined a young person as between 14 and 18. There is no consistency in definition but as the period of schooling has been extended childhood has been carved up. It is possible at least to recognize the stages of baby, infant, junior, adolescent and student.

This recognition, extension and differentiation of the period of dependency is the concern of law and commerce as well as social welfare and education. The United Nations have adopted a Declaration of the Rights of the Child. Social scientists refer to teenage, youth, adolescent and student cultures. The generation gap appeared in literature. Some leisure and luxury trades are focussed on the market among young persons. In many pre-literate societies the most marked elements in social organization are age groupings, so that males of similar age together acquire the same status as they get older. Thus Gulliver (1963) found that among the Arusha of Tanganyika, boys of six to twelve years old were circumcised together and then progressed as a group through the six stages from youth to retired elder. But in no pre-literate society is the age of dependency stretched out, and there is a quick transition from youth to adult often marked by tests and initiation rites. There is no 'in-between' stage where youth has an ambiguous status.

This extension of the period of dependency with modernization has come as the age of physical maturity has dropped. Children mature quicker physically yet take on adult responsibilities later. Tanner (1961), using data from Norway, reports that menstruation started at 17 in 1858, but at 13·7 in 1950. Earlier sexual development has accompanied delayed granting of adult rights. These changes make it very difficult to make comparisons across time and bring rapid redundancy to manuals of advice to parents and teachers.

The scope of the family
All generalizations about changes in the family should be treated with extreme caution because of the variety which exists at any one time. The first set of changes revolves around the diminished importance of kin. Laslett (1965) has argued that survival in Stuart times was only possible within a family. Usually this meant leaving the family into which you were born and serving in another until marriage. Boarding out and apprenticeship was usual among the rich as well as the poor. Laslett has stressed that there was considerable mobility in the Stuart period. Moving to find a place in a family household gave a chance of survival in a near subsistence economy and guaranteed a place in a network of supportive and supporting responsibilities.

The trend for the extended family of kin to be succeeded by the nuclear family of husband, wife and children does not mean that kin are now unimportant. Young and Willmott (1957) still found kinship as a factor in getting a job in Bethnal Green in the 1950s. Rosser and Harris (1965) found the extended family still going strong in South Wales in the 1960s. Both Rosser and Harris, and Willmott and Young (1960) in a study of Woodford found that kinship was also a persisting influence among the middle class.

However, the diminished contact with kin and the decreased variety of ages and types within the same household is marked when the Twentieth Century is compared with the past. The Stuart household could consist of married children, grandchildren, elderly relatives, cousins, unmarried aunts and also servants, lodgers and apprentices. Laslett found that in 1676 there were 277 persons in Goodnestone next Wingham in Kent. Of these 179 lived in 29 households of the gentry or yeomen while the remaining 98 persons lived in the 33 households of tradesmen, labourers and poor men. There were 52 servants out of these 277, born into poor homes but serving in the richer homes. This household structure of extended kin, lodgers and servants gave place only slowly to the modern nuclear type. Anderson (1971) found that in Preston in 1851 the number of kin, lodgers and servants in households was still in excess of the modern figure. The structure of rural families seemed to have changed little in two centuries.

The transition to a less extended household meant that parents took more part in the upbringing of their own children. Children were now not only taken into account, but increasingly became the centre of family life and concern. This increased interest was a symptom of more important changes. Up to, and throughout the Seventeenth Century, it was the standing and success of the family that mattered, not that of individuals. This can be seen most clearly in the arrangement of marriage, not on the basis of love, but for its benefit to the families concerned. But by the Seventeenth Century a stress on individual promotion, individual happiness and individual striving was detectable. Individualism was to become a major social force, particularly among the growing urban commercial classes.

There was an accompanying change in the organization of education. Apprenticeship, rather than schooling, had provided an education for the people in medieval time. Apprenticeship at its best was a genuine education, in which the master taught the child not only the skills of a trade but the way he should live. Contracts of apprenticeship, usually lasting seven years, made the master responsible for the child's welfare, under the supervision of the guilds. The apprentice lived with the family of the master.

While apprenticeship continued, and became the subject of further legislation in the Elizabethan Poor Law, schooling became an alternative in the towns. Jordan (1959) has shown that in the century before 1660, private philanthropy had established a system of grammar schools in the towns that provided opportunities unequalled until the Twentieth Century. This was not just apprenticeship for the poor and schools for the rich. Even the aristocracy had sent their children to court. All social ranks had sent their children to other families to be trained. The increasing number of schools must have reinforced a more individualistic, less familial view of life, and increased the concern of parents for their own children.

Only in the Nineteenth Century did schooling come to be the most important agency in formal education. Apprenticeship and domestic service, particularly when combined with strong influence by the Church were the main educative forces with the family for passing on skills and ensuring morality in pre-industrial Britain. Smith (1931) using the probably unreliable figures of Nineteenth Century writers has shown that Sunday schooling remained more important than full-time schooling until well into that century. The spread of schooling for the populace was another indication of a new way of life, individualistic, more mobile, in which children learned much that was unknown to their parents.

Victorian England contained an army of vagrant children no longer secured within stable households. The orphans, vagrants, young delinquents and deserted had to be taken off the streets and schooled. But the workhouse, industrial reformatory and ragged schools of the Nineteenth Century were only catering for those children not under parental control in the same way that the elementary schools catered for the rest of the common people. All were primarily concerned with the morals of the child, with discipline and good behaviour, rather than academic education. Indeed, Silver (1965) has shown how attempts to educate the poor beyond their literacy, were often vigorously opposed.

Some idea of the situation at the beginning of the Victorian period can be gauged from the reports of the Manchester Statistical Society (1834, 5, 8). In the Manchester area about a third of the children had never been to a school. Only about half of those on the school books ever attended at any one time. Sickness, poverty and the death of parents added to the uncertainty of trade to leave many children on the streets. The teachers were untrained. In the

Manchester and Salford National School there was one master and one mistress to 260 boys and 160 girls. The elementary schools were expanding to take over the upbringing of many children for whom family life had broken down.

A similar development in schooling can be seen among the middle class. Musgrove (1966) has stressed that sending a child to school would be a sign of failure in the parents of the rich. Schooling was unnecessary if the family was competent. In the last half of the Nineteenth Century schooling became more essential for the children of the middle class. The family could no longer provide new professional, commercial and technical skills. Indeed, Banks (1954) has argued that the limitation in family size which started among the middle class in the last quarter of the Nineteenth Century was due to an attempt to pay for the schooling of the children in a period when domestic help was becoming more expensive. In all social classes therefore the family lost some of its responsibility for the upbringing of children to the school. As in many other areas of life, a division of labour was appearing in the socialization of the young.

The spread of schooling through the social classes is an indication of the other major change in the scope of the family. It was not only shools that were needed to cope with the new situation in the Nineteenth Century towns. Smelser (1959) has traced the start of many supports for the working class family to the period between the Factory Acts of 1833 and 1847 when the family could no longer work as an economic unit and parents were in the factories but their children were excluded. By the end of the Nineteenth Century the full range of social services to support the family was visible.

The scope of the family has been restricted. The social services have taken over or supplemented many tasks that used to be done within the family. This is not necessarily a weakening of family influence. The social services are in many ways the support of the nuclear family in urban, industrial society. But the family is no longer self-sufficient and in one important sense has declined in its influence. Modern societies are geographically and socially mobile. The occupations of children are decreasingly determined by their parents and increasingly by schooling. The role of kin in the granting of adult status has decreased. The school prepares children for a changing world and provides opportunities, however unequal, for competition for access to many of the high prestige occupations.

Behind these changes in the context of the socialization of the young lie changes that can not be investigated directly yet are crucial in understanding the problems that are taken up later. In the last two centuries children have had to learn new concepts of time, space, cause and effect. The phases of the moon, harvest time, sun up or down are no longer accurate enough and time is now measured to the second by watches strapped to our wrists. Mileometer, ruler and micrometer replace the distance a man could plough or walk in a day, his height or the length of the joints of his fingers. Destiny, God's will, fate, witches and magic are replaced as causes by scientific explanation. The world facing the child, particularly the range of knowledge that now exists, has created a different and rapidly changing context for socialization.

CHAPTER TWO

The context of socialization in contemporary society

THE EVIDENCE FROM history and anthropology not only indicates the wide range of practices in socialization but the tendency for these changes to be accelerated during modernization. This chapter deals with the major factors underlying socialization in contemporary Britain. It is not primarily concerned with social class differences although these are the outstanding feature of the rearing of the young. Evidence on this can be found in Chapters seven, eight and nine, or in Klein (1965). Here there will be only a snapshot of a fast changing scene. Indeed, not only is the rate of change increasing, but more and more resources are being invested in research and innovation to ensure acceleration. Beliefs practices and knowledge are all subject to rapid redundancy. That which was good enough for father is highly suspect for the son.

The contemporary context of socialization is formed by the complex nature of modern, urban, industrial societies. Behind the evidence lie two profound changes. First, large numbers of people are now supported at high densities in conditions of material prosperity. Second, there is a widespread belief that the conditions of life are under human control and are subject to improvement by human ingenuity. It is not just increased affluence that is important, for this is often expended on satisfying needs that have been artifically stimulated. It is the combination of improved means for controlling the environment and satisfying human needs, coupled with the faith and will to exercise control. The accumulation of evidence on socialization is both a symptom of this faith and a means for exercising control.

The decreasing impact of death
Today few children experience death in the family or killing epidemics in the community. The Royal Commission on Population (1949) found that the rapid improvement had come in the Twentieth

Century. In the period 1838 to 1854, 135 girls out of 1,000 died before they were one year old. This infant mortality rate changed little until 1900. Today it is around 20 per thousand. Around 1850, 323 females would survive to 65. By 1942, 707 were surviving. If children experience death at all it is among the old.

Behind this fall in death rates has been a medical as well as a nutritional improvement. The contagious diseases which were the big killers in the Nineteenth Century have been controlled. Barnett (1961) has pointed out that cholera is now called a tropical disease yet a single infected well near Piccadilly Circus resulted in 485 deaths from this cause in ten days in Victorian London. Smallpox, typhus, enteric fever, measles, whooping cough and diphtheria are no longer mass killers.

Decreasing family size
The average number of children per family declined after 1900 alongside the fall in infant mortality. The Royal Commission on Population (1949) using evidence from the Fertility Census of 1911 found that the average number of children per family in the 1860's was around six. For those married between 1925 and 1929 it was 2·19. Among working class families, 43 per cent had over seven children in the second half of the Nineteenth Century but for those married in 1925 the percentage with over seven had fallen to two per cent.

This decline has been due to deliberate family limitation, starting among the middle class in the Nineteenth Century and slowly spreading. However, The Family Census (1949) for the Royal Commission on Population found that the greatest reduction in family size was among the white collar workers and the smallest among the semi-skilled and unskilled workers. Completed family size for professional and clerical workers was around 2·0, but was 3·76 for unskilled workers. Only five per cent of clerical workers' families contained more than three children, but this applied to 34 per cent of unskilled workers.

It was not just that the poorer parents tended to have larger families that was to be a continuing source of problems in the affluent society after 1945. In Chapter six there is an account of continuing differences, not only in the material conditions of life, but a tendency for the social services, particularly education, to be used most fully by the various middle class groups. People in the Twentieth Century live longer, are fitter, wealthier and supported by more comprehensive social services. But the rise in overall standards has not removed the deprivation of unskilled workers compared with the rest. It is this relative deprivation that is now a major concern of those seeking equality of opportunity in social policy.

The position of women
Falling death reates, better health and smaller families have transformed the lives of women. This is probably the most striking single development in the last half century and in the socialization of the young. Behind this trend has been technological advances. Improvements in rubber technology facilitated family limitation, and the contraceptive pill has made family planning even more convenient. Sanitary and medical advances coupled with improved farming and nutrition lie behind better health. Plastic pants, rubber boots and synthetic materials have made the mother's life easier. Tinned food, gas or electric fires, detergents and washing machine or a launderette lighten other chores that exhausted our grandmothers.

Both Myrdal and Klein (1956) and Titmuss (1963) have compared the life of the average woman in the mid-Nineteenth and the mid-Twentieth Centuries. They now live longer, marry earlier and complete their smaller families quicker than their grandmothers. Titmuss describes the average married woman in the 1890s as having ten pregnancies and spending 15 years nursing a child in the first year of life. She could expect to live until 65 having spent a third of her adult life over 20 bearing and rearing children. She would have had 12 years left after the children had left school, usually worn out, ill and steadily declining.

Today only four years are spent in pregnancy or nursing a child under a year old. The woman can expect to live until 77 having spent only seven per cent of her adult life bearing and rearing her two children. Even with the raising of the school leaving age there will still be 36 years left with the children off her hands, not to decline away, but to enjoy and she is also more likely to work. For many women today life does actually begin at forty, not start to end. They are the largest single source of available labour and will easily out-live their husbands. Moreover, far from feeling guilty about having small families and preserving their health, women today are pressed not to be selfish and exceed the norm of two children and are encouraged to become glamorous grandmothers. These changes have been accompanied by changes in the part played by fathers. Taconis (1969) reports not only fathers helping to bring up their children, but actually enjoying it.

The other dramatic change in the life of women is that having raised her children she can take up or go back to work. Among the sample of married women workers studies by Jephcott, Seear and Smith (1962) the most frequently mentioned reason for working was to raise their standard of living. But they also felt that going out to work made them more interesting wives. Both Douglas and Blomfield (1958) and Yudkin and Holme (1963) found that there was no apparent ill effect on children when their mothers went out to work. The reason for this may have been that the working mothers were better organizers that those who remained at home. Moore (1967) found that as long as the children were over three when a stable substitute was first found so the mother could go to work, there was little difference in emotional adjustment from those with whom the mother stayed home. Indeed, the experience of a substitute seemed to toughen the boys and make them less anxious.

The professionalization of socialization

The work of the family in socializing the young has been pro-gressively supplemented by social services, particularly schooling. All these services spread professional views about correct ways of bringing up children. Health visitors, antenatal clinics, midwives, family doctors, obstetricians, hospital services spread the message. It appears on the walls of doctors' waiting rooms, in clinics and street hoardings. It is spread through newspapers, magazines, television and radio. It is wrapped up in advertising, spread in the play group, nursery class, infant and junior school. It is always reinforced by the stress put on the importance of the first few years of life for future development.

The common elements in this message are of a bright, sanitary, well-nourished and healthy family of two children. But there is often contradiction, not only in the content of the messages, but between the message and the conditions in which many families have to live. The consequence is a recurring one of the advice getting home only to those who need it least. The professional view of socialization is not only often out of tune with circumstances, but changes very fast. Indeed, the history of advice to parents in the Twentieth Century suggests either farce or a switch in the nature of children from monsters to angels within a few decades. It makes the confidence of the experts even more incomprehensible.

In the Mothercraft Manual of 1928, Liddiard suggests using splints on the legs of the child before putting to bed if there is a tendency to masturbate. This was however a more relaxed view than the 1914 United States Children's Bureau's Child Care Bulletin which recommended tying the child's feet to opposite sides of the crib and pinning the nightgown sleeves to the bed to make sure that no enjoyable self-tickling occurred. Probably the most influential writer in England was Sir Truby King who recommended a Spartan regime dominated by the clock. Regularity was the key, regardless of the child's cries.

These were professionals backed by psychological evidence. Watson (1928) one of the most influential psychologists of his day, condemned the habit of mothers kissing and cuddling their children because it satisfied a sex-seeking urge in her. Watson's advice was never to hug, kiss or have a child on the lap. The advised stance was objectivity. The mother was to learn to keep away from the child. The ideal condition would be care from a well-trained nurse, changed every week to avoid any attachment being established with the baby.

Wolfenstein (1950-51) has traced advice on child-rearing in North America through the successive Bulletins on Infant Care of the United States Government's Children's Bureau. In 1914 when it was first published the child was seen as a parcel of all that was dangerous, rebellious and sexually undesirable. If these impulses were not eliminated the child would be wrecked for life. The mother had to be vigilante and warder, relentlessly battling against the child's efforts to suck his thumb or tickle his privates. However, by 1942 the message to parents had changed remarkably. Erotic pleasure now seemed to be of little concern and the mother was encouraged to enjoy herself with her children.

Wolfenstein has called this change the emergence of fun morality. Parents in the 1945 version of the Infant Care Bulletin were promised that having children would make them happy together, keep them young and give them fun. From being made to feel guilty for even hugging your child in the 1920s you were to be guilty only if you did not find parenthood one long delight in 1945. The most influential writer on both sides of the Atlantic since 1945 has been Spock. His message (Spock, 1945) was relax, enjoy yourself, do what comes naturally, be friends with your child and let him enjoy himself. However, the message of Spock has also changed. In Problems of Parents (Spock, 1962) he admitted that in his earlier books he was conforming to a trend and now wished for less casualness and a return to good manners.

This contradictory and fluctuating professional advice has also occurred in advice to teachers. Streaming was recommended as progressive in the 1930s but condemned as reactionary in the 1950s. Look and Say methods of teaching reading arrive with acclaim and depart in suspicion. Child-centred education sweeps into prominence, is enshrined officially (Plowden Report, 1968) and immediately comes under attack (Dearden, 1968; Peters, 1969).

The secularization of socialization
The disappearance of God and the Devil, Heaven and Hell, Salvation and Damnation from advice given to parents and teachers does not necessarily mean that religious influences have waned. Many writers such as Inglis (1960) have shown how the influence of the churches was never strong in many industrial towns if the evidence of the 1851 Religious Census was reliable. On the other hand the churches have played an important part in shaping every major Education Act (Cannon, 1964).

The important feature here is the extent to which religious influences are likely to be felt by children either directly through membership of religious organizations or through the religious attitudes of parents. Martin (1967) reviewing the available evidence concludes that there is support for Sunday schooling among parents but that actual attendance has fallen. In the Nineteenth Century a majority of children went to church or Sunday School. In 1957 one parent in two claimed to send their children to Sunday School, but in 1964 only one in seven children attended regularly. Similarly Scouts, Guides and other youth organizations often attached to churches have come under pressure.

Decline in the attachment of children to the churches is important because they may never come under the influence of religion at any point in their lives. This situation is similar within social work. Charity in the Nineteenth Century was motivated by, and pervaded with, religious attitudes. But the professionalization of social work and its concentration within large specialist organizations has removed one other channel of religious influence.

The organization of schooling
The experience of children in school has been influenced by the same set of factors that have changed socialization within the family. By the end of the Nineteenth Century elementary schooling had been made compulsory. In the Twentieth Century the elementary school was made part of a genuine school system, supplemented by a variety of other services that would, by 1970, be recognizable as the beginnings of a genuine system of education. This consists of the schools at the centre, surrounded by a number of services provided by government, industry and the mass media. Once again there has been a proliferation of specialist units concerned with socialization. These developments make it increasingly difficult to detect where schooling finishes and where the remaining agencies of education begin.

Probably the outstanding development in the Twentieth Century has been the extension of the time that children spend in school. This has been partly due to raising the age at which children can leave school, but has also occurred through voluntary staying on. Every increase in the age at which the children leave school relaxes the pressure on primary schooling. Since 1945 the key age for selection has shifted slowly from 11 to 18. As the eleven plus examination disappeared, there was a tendency for streaming and the more academic elements in primary schooling to also disappear. The freedom to introduce learner-centred schooling has been created by lengthening the time spent in school and consequently reducing the amount of learning that has to be packed into the early years.

Schooling like family life, has also been affected by the increased interest in childhood. Child-centred schooling means just this. The child is seen to learn best if his needs are satisfied, if he can go at his own pace, if he can pursue his own interests, and if the learning experiences that are organized for him are adjusted to his stage of development. The one consistent policy of the teachers' unions is the reduction of the size of school classes. This policy aims at increasing the attention that can be given to individual children. This policy is pursued even though the evidence suggests that academic results are better in larger classes (Shipman, 1972). The policy is based on the major item of faith in education. Children are seen as containing within them, not only the ability to learn, but the ability to direct that learning themselves. The parallel with the direction of advice given to parents in the Twentieth Century is obvious. Children are at the focus of the high hopes of both parents and teachers.

In a similar way the teacher is exposed to advice by professionals. The time devoted to education by the mass media of communication increases yearly. The amount of money given for research in education and the resources devoted to curriculum development also increases. The teacher, like the parent, is at the centre of much advice, often contradictory, but also stressing the same message that what matters is knowledge of the child. The contrast between the modern, open-planned primary school and the Board school built at the end of the Nineteenth Century is as striking as the contrast between modern, permissive ways of bringing up children in the family and the repressive methods that were used by our grandparents. While there are great differences between the experiences of different social groups, the material environment of children is now less often threatening or unpleasant.

Even though we cannot gauge the effects of our actions on children we have nevertheless organized for them an early life in which little is left to chance. At its extreme in totalitarian regimes, this can be an attempt to produce adults who conform to a particular pattern of behaviour and belief. However the comparative studies of Paton and Beloff (1970) and Bronfenbrenner (1972) suggests that even without outright indoctrination there can be a combination of parent, peer and teacher that can push powerfully towards conformity, particularly where peer influences are organized in a para-military way. Even where parents may seem to be taking less direct part in influencing older children, and where peer activities are not mobilized to support a regime, there is still an organized and professional structure for socialization. If we are more individualistic than the Russians this is a consequence of early experiences as well as of the continuing influence of the way our society is organized. There can be socialization for conformity or for individuality. Each has its credits and debits. Each rests on a different interpretation of the way social life should be constructed.

CHAPTER THREE

Socialization

THE PARENTAL APPRECIATION of the physical marvel of the new-born baby is soon accompanied by a realization of its inconveniently biological nature. Yet a year later the baby has become visibly social, recognizing parents, responding to others and gaining responses from them (Schaffer, 1971). Sometimes around the third year of life, food and drink are consumed in a civil manner and bowels and bladder are under control. So are the child's emotions. Behaviour is visibly male or female. Social class differences in abilities are appearing (Hindley, 1965). The infant has learned to adjust his behaviour to that of others and to communicate his wishes to them. He can now interact socially in a predictable way.

Similar, if less dramatic, changes recur. The child first entering the reception class of the infant school is uncertain of the way he should behave. In a short time he is playing his part confidently, both in relation to the class and to the teacher. Outside the class-room he learns to play a part in various school groups. In school, as in the family, the child has learned to participate in social activity.

The young child is socialized once his behaviour takes account of the expectations of others, as well as of his own feelings. The first few years of life are crucial. In learning to communicate and in becoming alert to the expectations of others the child not only becomes a social being, but acquires an image of himself as a person and of the world around him. Socialization occurs throughout life whenever an individual participates in a new social situation. But it is the socialization of the child that provides the base from which, later, novel situations will be interpreted. In the early years of life the child learns to see the world, and his part in it in a consistent way.

There are three types of study concerned with child development. The first concentrates on problems of maturation and the stages of development. The second is concerned with the way the child learns.

The focus used in this book is on agencies of scoialization such as the family and school, on the social interaction that occurs within them, and the impact of that interaction on the child. None of these approaches is complete by itself. For example, maturation and learning cannot be separated. Social interaction is dependent on an adequate command of language, emotion and body. The contribution of psychologist and sociologist are complementary not conflicting.

The view of the process of socialization used here will be stated in seven propositions.

1. *The child faces a packaged world*

The most obvious feature of the world that faces the child is that he has played no part in its production. He can interact with those people who interpret it for him, but he has played no part in deciding the nature of the roles which others will expect him to play and will help him to learn. The child's world is given to him. He stops being a child only when adults have been satisfied that he has learned to behave in their habitual, predictable ways.

This packaged world which faces the child is the product of social interaction. Life can only persist if humans can predict the actions of others, and themselves act in ways that are predictable. Habits, customs, rituals and institutions arise during this social interaction. But, once established, these patterns of behaviour become ready-made blueprints for succeeding generations. The child is not just born into a world of adults. He is faced by expectations that have been laid down by many generations before his.

To the child the established patterns of behaviour appear as established facts. This world appears unalterable and coercive. There is no possibility of changing it and the adults offer few alternatives. The child has to internalize this world in order to interact with those who are already in it. The roles of male or female child, brother or sister, and so on are clearly defined. Socialization is the process wherein the child takes the identity which is associated with these roles and the blueprint that faces the child becomes part of him.

The learning of a language is typical of this process. The child has to learn it in order to interact and survive. It is through the language, a social invention, that the child comes to see the world.

He cannot alter it. He cannot interpret his part in the world except through it. It constrains him. It is simultaneously the means through which he becomes an interacting, predictable human, and the means through which he comes to internalize the world as he finds it.

Parents, teachers and other adults responsible for children rarely question the blueprint they are handing on. They too have been socialized to see the existing order as legitimate. This is why mis-behaviour on the part of children is often viewed as intolerable. The child is not just being naughty in not behaving according to the blueprint. He is behaving irrationally. To the adults the message they are passing on is objective truth. Failure to heed it is often seen as absurd, unpredictable and unreal.

Berger and Luckmann (1967), from whom this view has been taken, summarize it as follows: 'Society is a human project. Society is an objective reality. Man is a social product.' It is because society is a human product that the changes described in Chapters one and two can take place. Each new child learns a part of the existing culture, part of the existing stock of knowledge. Socialization is not a stereotyping, for each child will learn a different combination of roles that will always have been defined in slightly different ways. Consequently human interaction always involves fresh interpretation and negotiation. This increases as humans accelerate the changes in their material world. Each generation changes the blueprint before handing it on to the next. Fundamental changes may now be coming within the lifetime of one generation. All that is certain is that human interaction is only possible if behaviour is predictable. This predic-tability is ensured through socialization.

2. *We learn from the expectations of others*

At any one time an individual occupies a number of positions or statuses in relation to other people. As a brother, a sister, a son, a daughter, a boy, a girl, a friend and in many of the other positions through which a person relates to others there will be expectations about the behaviour that is appropriate. These expectations define the role that is expected of persons of the particular status. The expectations do not form a straitjacket. There is rarely agreement over the way all little girls should behave in all circumstances. Advice to parents and teachers on the ways to treat children differ widely between authors. In every position that the individual finds himself there will be conflicting expectations, obscure and very loose expectations. For all but the baby there is usually a chance of exploiting this lack of agreement.

3. *We learn who we are by treating ourselves as objects*
The perspective used here is a simplified version of that developed by Mead (1934). Humans are not only alert to the expectations of others and sensitive to clues about the opinion of others about their performance. They also have the ability to treat themselves as objects. 'How am I doing?' is often asked. The individual does not only assess himself but throws out clues to others and learns about himself from the responses. He is capable of taking the role of the other, trying out different roles, identifying and internalizing. These are all active searches by the individual for roles that suit him. This objective view of the self is built-up by concentrating on the responses of an often small number of other people. Parents, teachers and friends can not only be important to the child because interaction with them is frequent but through the emotions that are sometimes involved. The responses of some adults become very important to the child, they bring pain or pleasure. There are significant others, often used as models as well as guides. Again this is not a passive reception of an offered model. For every significant other there are insignificant ones. The choice is made by the learner from choices that may not be limited to actual persons but may even extend to fictional characters. But in all cases the self is built up from social interaction, whether in work or play.

Most of the situations which the individual defines and makes meaningful are social. Action is based on the individual's inter-pretation of the actions of others. Thus individuals behave towards each other according to the way each sees the actions of others. The clues which the individual uses for his interpretation of the situation are sorted out in his mind. The future is anticipated as a basis for action in the present. Similarly the past can be summoned up as a basis for present behaviour. The whole process of interaction through which the individual builds up a self image and decides on appropriate behaviour is therefore symbolic. The most distinctive human characteristic is this ability to manipulate symbols, to summon up the past, extend the present and predict the future. The most important set of symbols are incorporated into language. Writing, language and image making are keys to the formation of human personality. The child paints his own picture of the world, but the models and the means of expression are given to him.

4. *Learning is active*

The essential feature of the theory just outlined is that the individual is not the product of forces over which he has no control, but is an active agent, not only in deciding on his own behaviour, but in interpreting the situations in which he is involved. The individual plays a part in determining his own self image. Very young children may just imitate, but with age the existence of a self image enables the individual to interpret the situations that he is in, in his own way. As soon as the infant sees himself as an individual he can direct his own behaviour.

The active intervention of the individual in the learning situations in which he is involved is based on accumulated experience. The young child in the family is unlikely to find any great discrepancy between past and present experiences. But in school he may find interpretation difficult as his past experience may not have prepared him for new social situations. The child's ability to learn and even his image of himself may be hampered by the lack of fit between the situations organized by the teacher and those he has experienced in his own family or local community.

5. *Socialization is a two-way process*

The most usual view of socialization is of a learner being exposed to the expectations of others and responding to them. Rewards and punishments are used to inhibit behaviour not approved by the socializer and to encourage those which are approved. But socialization occurs through interaction between individuals. The activity of the learner consists not only in interpretation but in intervention. As the learner responds to clues presented by others, he presents them with clues. They learn with him.

This two-way learning process has many important implications. First, it means that learning situations can range from those in which there is no room for the learner to influence the teacher, to those where there is give and take. Parents are often uncertain how to behave in a novel situation. They are alert to any clues which their children may give. They are on the look out for the way children are feeling, thinking and learning. They adjust their own behaviour towards the child on the basis of these clues. They may check them against the advice given in books, on television and radio, and by social workers. It is often difficult to see who is bringing up whom in a family with a new baby. The child is not only at the centre of attention, but is continually initiating behaviour in the adults.

Teachers, particularly when new to the job or on teaching practice, are often in classroom situations for which their past experience or training turns out to be an inadequate preparation. Finlayson and Cohen (1967) and Shipman (1967) have shown how student teachers are faced with contrasting expectations from college and school. But experienced teachers are also faced with novel experiences as schooling is changed from what Bernstein (1971) calls the collection curriculum towards that he has labelled integrated. As traditional content and methods are replaced by open-ended learning situations the teacher has to become more sensitive to the children in order to detect the appropriate next step. Child-centred schooling and liberal child-rearing practices force the teachers as well as the parents to learn more from the children.

There is a whole spectrum of possibilities. At one end the baby is in no position to bargain with his parents but the adolescent is frequently able to negotiate from a position of strength, supported by his peers. Similarly the junior school child has to take without question many of the instructions of the teacher, but the university student may insist on his views being considered. In most situations the actions of the socializer is at least limited by the active participation of the learner in the social interaction involved. Even a dictator cannot push a subject people too far. Only when human personality is destroyed can men be treated as animals without rights.

The negotiation and manipulation that take place during interaction have been extensively studied by Goffman (1968). Even in institutions with the most rigid rules governing the action of inmates there is till a process of negotiation. Not only do those under authority twist the rules but those in authority are party to this distortion. It is an unwritten contract which enables the inmate to establish some small area of freedom for himself under otherwise intolerable conditions. It is also a bargain for the nurse, warder or teacher because their authority ultimately depends on the co-operation of those in their charge.

The consequence of the two-way nature of socialization is that the individual is not faced with a consistent, complete and impermeable system of controls over his learning. This freedom results partly from disagreements between the agencies of socialization involved. Family and school, church and state, welfare agency and mass communication, all press their own version of the good life and their own definition of the good human being. Consequently the individual is faced with a variety of conflicting learning experiences. Furthermore, there are many areas of life where there are no established rules. Moral codes may lay down principles but cannot give prescriptions which are to be followed in the multitude of dilemmas which face individuals.

There is therefore a balance between an extreme where all agencies of socialization are unified and another where there is no agreement. The former offers order through constraint, the latter chaos through licence. Most societies are organized somewhere in between. It would be wrong however to over-estimate the latitude in sociali-zation. However wide the scope for individual interpretation, there is sufficient similarity between all Englishmen or Frenchmen, or all Tibetans for a cultural blueprint to be detected. Individual differences are great, but there remain similarities between members of different groups, different nations, and different sexes that indicate a degree of constraint. Furthermore, part of socialization consists of learning values that lead the learner to believe in the rightness and normality of his way of life and to see the organization of his society as legitimate.

6. *Socialization is doubly selective*

It has already been proposed that the young child is faced with a world already organized and defined for him by adults or older children. The significant others do not however just reflect the world to him, but interpret it in advance. This is double selectivity, first an extraction from the existing stock of knowledge and then an interpretation by the significant adults. The child gets a package from a package and is often in no position to do anything but accept what is presented. Thus the world may seem a very different place to girl or boy, Northerner or Southerner, manual worker's child or white collar worker's child. But within each group there will also be discrepant views. Each child receives a different filtered version.

This version of the world, learned by the young child from important adults around him is liable to seem self-evident, legitimate, the only true version. It becomes the child's perspective. But it is both a view of the world and of the self. As the child learns a world-view he learns a self-view, also seemingly self-evident and therefore egocentric. Being able to see himself as an object brings the child self-knowledge and a knowledge of the way human affairs are arranged between people. There will be conflicting versions, but the programme for this socialization is organized. It is promulgated by social service, mass media, doctors, clergy and teachers. Above all it is organized through language which is the way knowledge is passed across the generations.

The selection and interpretation of knowledge is made a more formal programme in modern societies. Folklore can not carry the knowledge of a sophisticated technology or of a large-scale world. Law, religion, music, history and all forms of knowledge are written down, classified and transmitted by specialists. This increased specialization increases the number of models for the child to identify with and increases the chance of different versions of roles being available. Each child can sample different pools of knowledge. Socialization is less of a straitjacket in complex societies.

The school curriculum is a selection from this pool of knowledge. Philosophers such as Hirst (1969) have analysed gaps in the selection. Sociologists have concentrated on the injustice that has resulted from different selections of knowledge being given to different groups of children. They have been particularly concerned with the way schools reinforce the inequalities of life in the family through the selective application of different curricula (Young, 1971). Even where the object has been to promote a better deal for the less able the results may be to widen the gap between them and the more fortunate (White, 1969, Shipman, 1971, Young, 1971).

7. There are many diverse patterns of living
Anthropological studies of small-scale, pre-literate societies and
sociological studies of groups within modern, industrial societies
have shown great variation in what are normally considered basic
roles. There are societies where the behaviour expected of men is
similar to that expected of women here. Behaviour expected, or even
encouraged, among children in one place may be considered
immoral in another. Within any particular group socialization
ensures that behaviour is fairly predictable. But these predictions
break down when people from two different groups interact. Spencer
and Gillen (1927) found that the Keraki of New Guinea thought that
full maturity among boys could only be attained after a childhood of
passive homosexuality. Some may find my habit of not washing
my hands after a meal deeply disturbing. In many tribal societies
my insistence on bringing up my own children rather than those of
my sister would seem outrageous. Everyone tends to see their way
of living as right and proper. Ethnocentricity is world wide.

Individuals in the same society share enough of a common way of
interpreting the world, the universals, to interact with little friction.
Different groups within each society will have their own alternative,
characteristic set of meanings, but there is an overall cultural
pattern typified and carried by the language. Indeed, socialization
is often defined as the process through which individuals internalize
the culture. As a result, the perception by interacting humans of the
world is sufficiently common for each to see similar things in similar
ways. They speak the same language. They share common definitions
of time and space. They relate cause and effect in similar ways. Their
behaviour towards one another is predictable.

Studies of different cultures reveal very different ways of thinking
and acting. It is much more difficult to detect differences between
individuals when studying an alien group than it is to see the
difference between a group round the corner and your own. In the
chapters that follow on the family and the school in Britain, the
focus is on these differences. The teacher is one agent of socialization
among many. Children are exposed to many different and often
conflicting influences.They can interpret the action of the teacher
through their experiences with other socializing agents. Underneath
the broad similarities, socialization is like political bargaining. With

the exception of the very young child, who has little cultural baggage to carry around, the parties involved in socialization bring different interests with them. Socialization is often seen as a game. Teacher and learner may jockey for position to outwit the other and preserve their interests. But where children are involved, the game is always unequal. Behaviour within particular societies becomes predictable and ways of looking at the world become similar because the dice are always loaded in favour of the adults. The world is an external, objective reality to the child. Whether this is seen as the way conformity is made to triumph over individuality, or as the genuine basis of morality, it is the way successive generations are slotted into existing patterns. Social interaction depends on behaviour being predictable. A measure of conformity is the basis of living together.

Socialization into sex roles
These seven propositions can be illustrated through considering the way children come to know themselves as boys or girls. Nothing in this section eliminates the possibility that there are important biological determinents of sexual roles. But the emphasis is on learning in the first years of life. Hartup and Zook (1960) found that in the USA, children of three were aware of external differences between boys and girls. Between three and four the children rapidly adopted different types of role so that they are visibly acting as boys and girls by the time they enter school.

This early determination of sex roles indicates the given nature of the world to the child. The outward signs of this are pressures on boys to stand up for themselves, be brave and manly. Meanwhile little girls are taught to be ladylike. The toys that are bought, the frocks, the subtle differences in words, play, hugs, rewards, punishments and the example of mummy and daddy, surround the child with a world clearly distinguishing behaviour expected from boys and girls. The expectation of others, particularly those most significant to the child, are usually that the child shall adopt a clear, unambiguous sex role. It is against this background that the child must come to assess his own performance and learn about himself or herself as a person.

The early determination of sex roles is not accomplished through impact on a passive child. A child at play from an early age is

imposing his will on objects and other children. He defends his
version of events and his self-esteem. This is particularly noticeable
at the nursery school stage. Thus May (1963) says that children of
this age share objects with other children, use other children but
follow their own independent activity. By five years children's groups
in infant schools may be fully organized, with chiefs, subordinates,
technicians and diplomats (Haufmann, 1963). The learning is now
two-way. But this increased range of activities outside the home also
enables the children to teach their parents more about the changes
that are needed once the child is at school. As the child learns sex
roles he or she is also learning to interact with others and actively
negotiate the conditions of further socialization.

Although the child can progressively exert more independent
action as he grows older, he does this in a world in which sex roles
have been clearly differentiated and defined. For each child this is a
double selection of meanings. The relations between the sexes have
been organized in a particular way, but this organization is interpreted afresh for each child by parents and other adults. It is
packaged for the child through mass media, advertising, the organization of schooling and through story, song and fable. But the
parents select from these packages to present the child with their
version.

The argument of the Women's Liberation movement hinges
around this social determination of sex roles. The inequality between
the sexes is preserved through the definitions of man and woman.
The situation is justified by reference to inherited differences, but
there is no way of confirming that these play an important part,
compared with the definition of sexual roles that are culturally fixed
and reinforced by folklore, etiquette and the concealment of inequality by romanticism.

Support for this view that sexual roles are culturally, not biologi-
cally determined comes from anthropological studies. The most
famous and most striking comes from Mead (1964). The Arapesh of
New Guinea are unagressive, affectionate people who are indulgent
to their children. But women do much of the heavy manual work and
no distinctions are made between masculinity and femininity.
Women are expected to take the initiative in sexual and community
affairs as much as men. In another tribe in New Guinea, the

Tchambuli, where children are subject to stresses as they grow up, the adult sex roles are the reverse of ours. Women are seen as the reliable, self-sufficient and lusty ones, while men are seen as sensitive, vain and temperamental creatures.

Anthropological studies reveal remarkable variations of this type. Almost any social arrangements can be made to work, even to the extent of the man lying in after the birth of a child while the woman returns to the fields. However it would be wrong to exaggerate the variety. Barry, Bacon and Child (1957) using data from 110 cultures report that girls are normally taught to look after others and to be obedient, while boys were normally taught to be self-reliant and assertive. Where hunting, herding or a nomadic existence was practised, sex differences were very closely demarcated. As most militant women realize, equality between the sexes depends on a social organization that is low on competition and struggle for existence.

CHAPTER FOUR

The child and the family

THE FOCUS IN this chapter is on the family as chief agent in socializing children into basic social roles. Three cautions are necessary. First, the common characteristics of family life are emphasized, whereas the evidence that is available points to wide differences between the experience of children in families from different social classes. The second caution is that the family is not alone in socializing the young child. Many social roles for all but the very young child are learned from siblings or friends. Indeed, Newson and Newson (1968) found that one of the few aspects of child care in which there was little difference between the social classes was that there should be mixing with other children by the fourth year. This mixing was organized by the mothers despite the difficulties in the urban conditions of this study because it was seen as such a vital part of growing up. The third caution is that it is easier to find a relation between family circumstances and the behaviour of children than to say one causes the other, because socialization is a two way process.

Interaction in the family
In the last chapter socialization was seen as a process of interaction wherein roles were learned from the expectations of others, by the learner putting himself in the position of others in order to gauge his own behaviour and in which all those involved were learning. The interest of the family as an agency in socialization is that it provides unique kinds of interaction. In a world in which most human contacts involve us as specialists, the family remains the place where we are treated, and treat others, as whole persons. This deep knowledge of our kin in the family, and of their intimate knowledge of us can be the cause of discomfort as well as contentment. These feelings are a sympton of the unique nature and power of the family in socialization. At work, in school, while shopping and even when passing the time of day with neighbours we are interacting

with others who know only bits about us connected with particular skills or shared experiences of the same events or area. We usually know little about other people as persons and often the introduction of personal detail is resented as interfering with the particular business in hand.

Parents in particular have a very full knowledge of their young children. But the demands that are made on individuals in the family and the obligations they accept are also widespread. In contemporary Britain with re-housing, less exhausting working conditions and increased employment for women, the father is increasingly involved in this intimate interaction. Chapman (1955), Mogey (1956) and Willmott and Young (1960) all report that working class husbands tend to become more family-centred when there is a move from central areas to a new house, to suburbs or new estates. Newson and Newson (1963) found that only among unskilled manual workers was there a majority of husbands who did not participate to a high degree in helping with the children. This tends to be confirmed among the small sample of affluent workers investigated by Goldthorpe *et al.* (1969). These tended to become 'privatized', their lives revolving around family and home.

This trend to a home-centred family contrasts with the mother-centred families reported in central urban areas by Willmott and and Young (1957) in Bethnal Green in the 1950's, and in Mogey (1956) in Oxford. In the traditional mining area studied by Dennis *et al.* (1956) the men spent most of their time with their mates, not their wives. The important point here is that as the husband helps with the children, works around the house, goes shopping or for a walk with his children there is a new element in socialization. The child now learns his roles within families where the parents share tasks and leisure.

If the intimacy of contemporary family life is seen alongside the small size, the one family house and the participation of the father, the importance of the changes since industrialization can be appreciated. So far we know few of the consequences for children. The evidence we have suggests that it is within this small group that the personality is formed, for better or worse. On one side writers like Fletcher (1962) argue that the modern family fulfils its socializing functions satisfactorily. On the other side Leach (1967) argues that the intimacy is claustrophobic, creating excessive anxiety about the children and within them.

Unfortunately most research on socialization in the family has been confined to the effect on children not the effect of children. Walters and Stinnett (1971) reviewing 200 articles on parent-child relations in the 1960s conclude that few generalizations are possible without long lists of qualifications. Poor parent-child relations seem to produce anti-social behaviour and a negative self-image in the children. Children learn to interact in the family and there seems to be a difference between the middle class parents' use of reasons and appeals to guilt and the working class parents' more frequent use of physical punishment. But the context of family life must always be considered. Low income poor housing and large families tend to go together and children become a nuisance quicker than where there is more space and fewer children. Children learn through interaction in different contexts, involving different groupings of people not directly through the one way influence of parents.

The clue to the importance of stable, warm parental care for young children should lie in studies of varieties of broken homes. But Wootton (1959) has attacked most of this work as inadequately defined and controlled. The original thesis of Bowlby (1951) that personality disturbance was likely to result from depriving the child of the affection of the mother was shown by Ainsworth (1962) to need elaboration. Since then the evidence has been conflicting. Cowie *et al.* (1968) support the Bowlby thesis that maternal deprivation occurred frequently among deliquent girls. But many children from poor homes, broken families and who suffer extreme deprivation still grow up stable and non-deliquent. The safest conclusion is probably that stable and close relations with parents in the early years give the best chance of satisfactory personality development. Both parents seem to play a part, for Andrey (1960) showed that lack of paternal affection was more common among delinquents than their more law-abiding peers. This more general conclusion must be tempered by the association between poor material conditions, family difficulties and delinquency and personality disorders. Indeed, both Wilson (1962) and Gibson and West (1968) report that low income and poor living conditions were the basic causes of trouble and that parental pathology and delinquency follow as a consequence. Poor relationships in the family are crucial, but they are often reflections of adverse material conditions which offer little scope for anything better.

The interaction within the family of the young child is not only intimate but intense. Parents and children communicate not only intellectually, exchanging ideas, judgements and sentiments, but emotionally, so that even factual communications may be loaded with love or hate. Furthermore, much of the communication in the family is non-verbal, based on an intimate knowledge of what a grunt, smile, a hug or a sigh means. Even before the child learns to talk he is communicating with his parents. Indeed in the most intimate moments of family life, be they full of love or hate, words can become superfluous.

This intimacy is intensified in the small modern family. Bossard and Boll (1966) have pointed out that there is a Law of Family Interaction. The number of personal interrelationships increases faster than any increase in the numbers involved. The modern four person family has six possible personal relationships, the eight person Victorian family had twenty-eight. This intensity in the modern family is accompanied by a stress on romantic love as the basis of marriage (Dennis, 1962). Indeed, with the passing of the family as an economic unit, the emotional attachment remains the strongest bond. Romantic love may ripen or decay, but the survival of the family rests on the husband and wife reaching some accommodation, comfortable or not. As with child-rearing, there is now a plentiful glossy literature on the need for the parents to create a warm, emotionally satisfying environment in the home. Family guidance has also been professionalized and secularized.

It might be expected that this emphasis on the parents' duty to secure a cosy nest for themselves and their children would put people off marrying or dramatically increase the level of divorce. But the evidence suggests that the promise of all kinds of family intimacy in a world dominated by large, impersonal organizations overcomes the perceived disadvantages. Statistics collected by the Registrar General (Social Trends, 1970) show that there was a steady trend towards marrying younger from 1901 to 1966, after which teenage marriages started to become less frequent. But the proportion that never married has also dropped during this century and there are no signs of this trend being reversed.The Registrar-General's Statistical Review (1968) shows that there has been a slight rise in the proportion of marriages ended by divorce since 1951 among those married less than ten years, but over 90 per cent of marriages remain intact and divorcees also tend to marry again in large numbers.

Family ritual and interaction

A ritual is not only a prescribed pattern of behaviour but one that is repeated in the same ways which come to be judged by those involved as right and proper. There is not just a building up of habits, but of feelings of right and wrong about the actions involved. Durkheim (1912) saw ritual as promoting crucial aspects of socialization. The most obvious gain for the group is that individuals feel more close to each other as a result of their common actions. This consolidation through ritual simultaneously divides the group off from others. They differentiate as they consolidate.

But the crucial socializing aspect of ritual comes from the combination of discipline and tradition that are involved. As the individual is involved in repetitive, emotionally loaded and morally sanctioned activity he is learning to accept constraints and learning the ways of the group. But this learning of the culture, the blueprint for living, via ritual, also brings a renewal of established practices. The social heritage, the construction of reality, is being acted out. When this is combined with the feeling of wellbeing and intimacy among those involved it becomes a powerful device for teaching old ways to newcomers.

Much of the rearing of young children in the family is deliberately organized to teach skills as quickly as possible. The child is made aware that his dirty pants are unwelcome. He is praised when they are clean. He is introduced to a potty, sat on it, shown brothers or sisters doing things the proper way. Even mundane actions can be ritualized. Indeed, the rigid schedules recommended by Truby King (1937) in the pre-Spock era laid the basis for the ritualization of child training. Meal times, bed time, getting up, shopping, Sunday outings, the Sunday meal, Saturday sport, Daddy's homecoming can be surrounded by habits that can not only be important for children but seen by them as proper. Their outrage if the sequence is broken indicates the hold that rituals have over them. But they are learning to get involved. From breast to bottle feed, nappy changing, through to the visits to relatives and the doling out of pocket money, the children are caught up in a number of repeated, intimate learning situations that build up a picture of the way of their world.

This description fits the material comfort of the middle class home rather than one where survival in the face of poverty takes priority. Bossard and Boll (1966) in a study of American families found that the number, variety and richness of rituals increases as you go up the social scale. But this is one of many differences in socialization that tend to reinforce each other and which will be considered in Chapters six, seven and eight. But if ritual is more a feature of the middle class home this is crucial for the upbringing of the children. The studies of Bossard and Boll at the Carter Foundation at the University of Pennsylvania suggest that habits are formed, emotional responses standardized, manners learned, leisure organized, co-operation practised and family continuity ensured through family rituals. What is really being said in this account is that ritual is an index of family integration and hence of the capacity of the family to socialise effectively. There are disadvantages as well as gains in this. Over-ritualized behaviour is inflexible, conformist and often in-tolerant of alternative patterns of behaviour. But it may be that the middle class family is capable of effective socialization because it has the room and leisure to engage in pleasing, comforting, gripping and potent ritual behaviour.

It is likely that the nature of family rituals has changed. Bossard and Boll (1950) studying families over the last 80 years in America noted trends in ritual from religious to secular, but no accompanying decrease in intensity. Rituals may become redundant quicker once their religious significance declines, but this may increase the pleasure taken in them. Finally the modern family with its relative prosperity and increased leisure has more opportunity for varied rituals than in the past. Again there may be a negative side to this intensity in the small family group. The mobile modern family in all classes seems to retain links with kin regardless of social class, but these contacts are occasional. The child learns within a tight-knit family group. This contrasts with tribal communities, parti-cularly with classificatory kin systems, where children are faced with numbers of adults taking responsibility for them as mothers, fathers and so on. It also contrasts with the extended household of rural areas in the Nineteenth Century. The consequences can only be guessed.

The parents socialize their children
Specific examples of social class differences in socialization will be found in Chapters seven and eight. Here one example is discussed to illustrate the significance of apparently trival aspects of family interaction and of the way parents, deliberately or not, influence the behaviour of their children in contrasting directions. Bernstein and Young (1967) in a study of 351 families have shown differences in the way mothers viewed the use of toys by their children. The middle class mothers were aware of the educational significance of toys and of their potential for learning about the environment and exercising control over it. The working class mothers were less likely to realize the educational significance of toys and tended to see them simply as a way of keeping the child amused and out of mischief. Jones (1966) had also found that middle class mothers chose toys more carefully for their properties as learning devices. The success of the educational toy sold by firms such as Galts, Abbotts and the Educational Supplies Association confirms this sensitivity of parents to the value of play. Parents thus secure the learning of important skills that will prepare for infant schooling.

However, Bernstein and Young also stress that the crucial factor seems to be not the toys themselves but the way they are presented by the parents with suggestions and illustrations of their potential. The toys became educational when they were introduced as part of a programme designed by the parents, often to illustrate some important feature of the material or social world. This illustrates the importance of the family context of particular activities. Little girls playing with dolls or little boys with toy cars can be guided towards play that is educational in the fullest sense and a crucial influence in the learning of basic social roles. But each activity is part of a whole family pattern that can range from close, warm co-operation to detached, uncomfortable chaos. Children are learning within this total context, not in isolated activities within it.

The children socialize their parents
So far the selection of research on relations between parents and children has been reported as if parental shortcomings or excellence, absence or illness, modes of play or expression influenced the way the children developed. But Kysar (1968) has pointed out that the influence could be just as well be from children's behaviour to parents' response. Disturbed children may wear out parents until they are in turn are disturbed. Maternal deprivation could be caused by the lack of affection of children towards their mothers. Rituals can be initiated by children yet involve the parents in children's play.

Many mothers must have been told that it was their anxiety that resulted in the depression, or disturbance or bed-wetting of their child. This is always over simplified as it is always impossible to predict the consequences for children of growing up in certain conditions. Even in the most disturbed families in the most delinquent sub-cultures many children grow up honest and stable. Within the same family the effects on different children will contrast. It may be that it is the bed-wetting or exhausting behaviour of children that first causes the parents to become disturbed. As most of the research starts with the assumption that parents bring up the children it is designed only to test the influence of the former on the latter. But the little evidence that has been collected from an interactionist perspective suggests that this is naive.

Most writers correctly stress the helplessness of the new born baby. Among the animals, man has the longest period of childhood and dependence. However much the parents plan for the arrival of the child, however much advice they receive, and however much they seek, the baby disturbs the established relations. But this is not merely the result of the demanding physical nature of the child. It is also the consequence of the rapidity with which the baby learns to demand attention and to manipulate relationships. Deliberate or not, the child's crying, smiles and gestures profoundly modify the lives of the parents and other siblings. Rheingold (1969) has said that the baby makes fathers and mothers out of men and women. The baby decides when he wants to eat, sleep, be moved or played with. He disturbs the day and night time routine of the parents. The final routine into which the child is trained within the family is a product of not only the parents' plans, but of the child's responses to them.

Remarkable illustrations of this kind can be found in the study of four-year-old children in an urban community by Newson and Newson (1968). In eight per cent of the cases studied, the mothers stayed with the child until he was asleep regardless of how long this was. Thirteen per cent of these four-year-olds slept in their parents' room. Twenty-six per cent of mothers were willing to chat to the child during the night. Sixty-six per cent of the mothers were willing to take the child into her bed. This is only one example of the disturbance to the life of the parents that the child can create. One mother even complained that she was getting fed up with sleeping four in a bed. A fidgety child with his two parents in the same bed, at four years old, had probably played a very large part in organizing a new family routine to suit his own needs.

Blood and Wolfe (1960) report that although most of the parents studied by them wanted children, their arrival caused a crisis. The baby caused financial hardship, loss of sleep, stopped the parents leaving the house and reduced the companionship between them. The series of crises and disturbances that children bring seem to result in an accommodation. Landis and Landis (1963) studying couples married twenty years conclude that they were neither very happy or very unhappy compared with childless families. Confirmation of this stability comes from the tendency for divorce rates to fall as the number of children in the family rises. Caution is again necessary. Parents with large numbers of children may be too poor or too exhausted to seek a divorce.

This view of socialization as interaction involves a contribution from children to the personality of the parents. Parsons (1955) has argued that children enable their parents to act out residual infantile tendencies in their personalities. Parents can engage in childish actions and simultaneously appear to be acting responsibly. Parents can play on the floor, lap up ice cream, be cowboys or Indians, keep goal for England and retain their appearance of sanity. Children can dictate a family regime, but this is not necessarily unwelcome to the parents. In a world where work, community, shopping and leisure tend to be impersonal and large scale, it may be important that children teach their parents to relax and play awhile.

CHAPTER FIVE

Children in the school

THE MOST revealing way of seeing how schools teach children new social roles is to compare behaviour in a newly arrived reception class in the infants' school with the same class some months later. Some of the children new to the school will be confident and sophisticated as a result of preparation by their parents, by elder siblings and through experience of play groups, nursery schools and classes. Others will be timid and fearful, reluctant to leave their mothers at the school gate. The transformation of this confused group into a smoothly operating infant class is the most significant clue to the work of the school in socialization. It is the triumph of the infant school teacher. In a very short time she has taught the children to see her not as a mother-substitute, caring for them as individuals demanding attention, but as a teacher responsible for them as members of a group. It also shows the power of the influence of children on each other. Those who know the ropes show the newcomers. They will also show new or student teachers what to do.

Whatever the emphasis put on academic work, the school is immersing children in routines that have been designed to promote behaviour approved by adults. But the school is not only an agent of socialization, it is organized to socialize children into its own routines. There is no automatic synchronization between these two socializing processes. The school may easily be teaching social behaviour that is inappropriate for the life which the children will lead outside.

Some indication of the importance of schooling can be gauged from the amount of time spent under instruction. About six hours per day, 1,200 hours per year, 12,000 hours before the first opportunity to leave school and about 16,000 hours for those who stay on through the sixth form are spent within this organization designed to socialize. Even more important, these hours in school are dominated by routines that have been developed to facilitate the smooth running of the school, an organization in a world of organizations.

The term 'hidden curriculum' has been coined to describe all the pressures and procedures that promote new forms of social behaviour. It has already been argued in England at least, that universal schooling developed to give the majority the discipline that was seen to be needed for a new kind of urban, industrial life. Much of this discipline, symbolized by school rules and encouraged on the games field or gym is still overt. Part of it is hidden, but no clear distinction can be made between the two. What is important is that the school, as an organization, is designed by specially selected adults, to promote forms of behaviour that they see as appropriate in children.

The formal organization may be designed to promote behaviour favoured by the teacher, but the children will organize themselves informally to soften the routine, make their life more comfortable and often frustrate the efforts of the teachers. Up to the age of seven, groupings among children may be unstable and there will be little support outside the school for opposition to the influence of the teachers. From eight or nine years on, groups will not only be more stable, but some will include those children who already feel themselves to be failures in the school and who are receiving support for alternative forms of behaviour from outside the school. Willig (1963) found that in the last two years of junior school life groups could be distinguished which contained those who had failed to achieve much and those who had been judged as successes. Hargreaves (1967) and Lacey (1970) have showed that later on in the secondary school, where streaming is more prevalent, this division between those in lower streams who reject the school and those upper streams who accept it becomes more marked. But the formation of groups within different ability levels is only one indication of a continual process through which children can actively influence the working of the school. Again, it is the interaction between those involved rather than a one-way process that is important. Even where a school appears to be oppressive and dominated by traditions, staff are constrained as well as pupils.

Teachers socialize the children
Some idea of adult expectations of children's behaviour can be
gauged by the changing architecture of primary schools as illustrated
in Seaborne (1971). To us the barracks built for elementary schooling in the last quarter of the Nineteenth Century appear mean. To
the late Victorians they were the ultimate in generosity. The high
brick walls which seal them off from the outside world tend to
confirm us in our views. We contrast this gloom with the modern
primary school, not only open to the outside, but built to use the
maximum amount of glass.

Inside the schools even more dramatic changes can be noticed. The
primary school classroom with rows of desks screwed to the floor,
with seats hinged to the desks, is now seen as repressive. The modern,
open-planned primary school may not have desks or fixed positions
for children. It may not even have classrooms.

These architectural changes reflect a change in the expectations
of adults towards children. It has come partly through a revision of
our ideas on the best way to learn. Even more important the changes
reflect the new view of childhood that was the subject of Chapter
two. In the last quarter of the Nineteenth Century, the struggle to
get children into school and to attend regularly was finally won
(Rubinstein, 1969). Schooling was to be experienced but not
necessarily enjoyed. Today it is not only that compulsion is less
common but that primary schooling at least is supposed to be
enjoyed. The fun morality applies in some schools as it does in the
family.

Ritual in school
Bernstein, Elvin and Peters (1966) have pointed to the activities
in the school that contribute to the transmission of values and
expectations as particularly prone to ritualization. Some rituals bind
the school together as a moral community by stressing its separate
identity. But such rituals also serve to relate the values in the school
to social, religious and political values outside it. Again socialization
into the school goes alongside socialization by the school. Other
rituals within the school serve to distinguish groups by age, authority,
sex or house. Bernstein, Elvin and Peters see ritual as the way values
are transmitted in the school. They see the part played by teacher-

directed ritual declining as traditional authoritarian regimes disappear in schools. But it will be replaced by pupil-directed rituals operating to promote new identities among the successful and the failures. Regardless of the accuracy of this prediction, its interest here is that changes in school organization are not predicted to lessen the part played by ritual, but to change its origins and consequences.

Here is a parody of the start of the school day. Within it are routines and rituals, clues, cues and symbols that surround and immerse children in school. However, they also surround teachers and the rituals are often the product of action by the children. In many public schools the rituals are so powerful that change is very difficult to organize. This may be the reason why public school headmasters tend to be appointed young and retire a few years later.

At 9 a.m. a blast on the whistle stops the children rushing round the playground in their tracks. Another blast gets them into lines facing the teacher with the whistle. Slight indications with one finger send successive classes into the school building. The children walk along the left hand sides of the corridors and line up outside their classrooms. A teacher arrives, nods her head and the children troop into the room and sit at their places. In the classroom there is a panoply of symbols: teacher's desk, blackboard, class notices, tables of stars accumulated by different houses, lists of marks, book-cases, piles of exercise books, forming, with many other objects, reminders of what schooling really means. The registration ritual follows. A bell rings and the children go through the undirected but systematic routine for going into the hall. Here the morning act of worship, combined with the school notices, provides a ritual incorporating both the sacred and the secular. These two ritual supports are clearly attached to the teachers by the physical arrangement of the hall. Going out of assembly, starting and finishing lessons, shifts in routine, having lunch, all the complicated procedures of the school day are accomplished with a minimum of words, a few bells, a few gestures and a lot of varied facial expressions. The children have learned the meaning of these symbolic actions and the responses that are expected of them. Even the subversive, parodied responses by dissident pupils tend to be counter-rituals.

Evaluation in school

The young child entering school soon discovers that his successes and failures are going to be measured in very precise terms compared with those he has previously experienced in the family. Schools employ a wide array of rewards and punishments in this evaluation. Some, such as examinations, tests, stars, house-points, and ticks in books are organized and deliberate. Others, such as privileges, responsibilities, smiles, frowns, down to smallest gestures may not be deliberately used as evaluation, but are such to the children. Even the child in the infant school soon realizes that his performance is being continually evaluated. Some schools make this more apparent than others, but to the child the meaning of schooling is the evaluation of achievement. This stress on evaluation is complicated by the part played by school in selection. This selection is partly for internal purposes. Children are promoted, demoted, given rights and responsibilities to ease the job of running a large organization. But the school also acts as the agency for sorting children out in preparation for the roles in which they will play as adults. This sorting out may be delayed until late in the school career, but sooner or later the process of differentiation occurs.

The most marked aspect of this evaluation in English schools has been streaming, organized within a system that has been selective in the secondary sector and continues to be so in higher education. The evidence on the effects of streaming does not enable any firm conclusions to be drawn about it as a means of improving the efficiency of teaching. While many small scale studies supported de-streaming or streaming on these grounds, the large scale study of primary schools by Barker Lunn (1970) was inconclusive. The crucial factor was the attitude of the teachers involved. If they supported one form of organization they would make it work. A follow-up by Barker Lunn (1971) confirms the importance of teacher behaviour, particularly in determining the attitudes of children to the school and hence motivation to learn.

The research on streaming has however uncovered important features of the effects of evaluation and placement into like-ability groups. Douglas (1964) found that there were 11 per cent more middle class children in upper streams in his sample of near 5,000 than would have been expected from their measured ability, and

20 per cent fewer in lower streams. In the same sample there was a tendency for all children in upper streams to improve their test scores between eight and eleven years if they were in upper streams, but in lower streams only middle class children improved their scores while the scores of working class children tended to fall.

The tendency for children in upper streams to improve performance and for those in lower streams to deteriorate suggests that evaluation by teachers influences the consequent performance of children. But this effect might not need overt action by teachers. Thus Nash (1971) observing teacher-pupil interaction in a non-streamed primary school found that the children were not fooled by efforts to camouflage selection. We have become rightly sensitive over the possible damage done by streaming and selection. But there are a variety of very often subtle means of selection within classrooms. Nash has shown that all the efforts of the teachers to prevent the children from identifying themselves as failures or successes compared with the rest of the class failed. Indeed, he argues that it may not be worth attempting to disguise from children how well they are doing. They know that schools are places where they are evaluated and are not easily fooled.

This sensitivity of children may account for the effects of streaming. Douglas (1964) found that less able children placed in upper streams improved their performance, but brighter children in lower streams showed the greatest deterioration. This suggests that children adjust to the labels, the evaluation that is made of them and that this can happen despite the efforts of teachers to conceal their judgements of the children. What seems certain is that it is rare for children to change streams. Douglas found that in his sample from eight- to eleven-year-olds, only 2·3 per cent moved up and the same proportion moved down. Daniels (1961) found that his small sample of teachers said that some 19 per cent changed each year. While these figures are not truly comparable they suggest that teachers overestimate movement. Overall, this evidence on streaming suggests that labelling children is a very effective way of altering their performance so that the validity of the label is confirmed.

Barnes (1971) has suggested that teachers prescribe the roles of children in the classroom through the language they use in their teaching. But this is not a passive reception by the pupils. Barnes

(1969) maintains that teachers teach within their frame of reference, but what they say is interpreted within the frame of reference of each child, often formed by very different social and personal experiences. Children make sense of what the teacher says by reference to their previous experience. If this is limited, little learning as planned by the teacher will occur. Furthermore, Barnes points out that the teacher controls the flow of information through his talk and questions, rarely giving the children the chance of asking the questions which would enable them to fit the content of the lesson into the experience they bring into the classroom.

The impression that teachers give to pupils is particularly important when it affects the child's self image. There is a long experimental tradition in America showing how different teaching styles can produce different responses among school classes (Amidon and Hough, 1967). More recently, Rosenthal and Jacobson (1968) have maintained that expectation of teachers is an important influence over the performance of pupils. The experimenters led teachers to believe that some children in their classes should spurt academically, although there was no actual evidence for this prediction. The teachers then produced the improvement in performance, even though the information on which their expectations were based was false. The most dramatic success was with younger children and there was little effect among those in the top two forms of this elementary school. There was no difference in the effect between different streams and little difference between the sexes. Rosenthal and Jacobson claim that later work has confirmed not only that the expectations of teachers can influence academic progress, but also influence the learning of motor skills.

This experiment has been widely quoted, and fits in well with evidence derived from studies of streaming which suggest that the labels which teachers attach to children influence the performance. It is one of many examples of self-fulfilling hypotheses (Rosenthal, 1966). However, as with all social scientific educational research, caution is needed. Replications of this experiment (Claiborn, 1969) have found no gains by the supposed 'bloomers' and teachers seem to be resistant to suggestions that certain children are performing below potential. The 'Pygmalion' study has been criticised as technically defective by Thorndike (1968). An investigation of the results presented by Rosenthal and Jacobson shows that the gains were confined to certain groups of children only. The failure of the replication to find even these, suggests that Rosenthal and Jacobson may have themselves been involved in a self-fulfilling hypothesis. A full account of studies relating pupil performance and the expectations of teachers can be found in Pidgeon (1970).

The alacrity with which educationalists have accepted the Rosenthal and Jacobson study and recommended that teachers go around smiling amicably on children is an example of the tendency for evidence to be accepted and used because it supports existing beliefs rather than because it is reliable. There is other evidence that suggests that the style of the teacher affects the performance and even the personality of the children. The most quoted experiment is that by White and Lippitt (1960) showing that different teaching styles produce different responses among groups of children. However caution is also necessary when reading secondary accounts of this work. The original has been severely criticised by Anderson (1963). There has been a progressive simplification and selection. Thus the original study contains evidence that authoritarian leadership leads to greater productivity (Lippitt and White, 1965). There is other evidence to suggest that democratic groups responded to frustration by attacking other groups (Lewin, Lippitt and White, 1967). There is a tendency to use evidence to support existing practices and to ignore any which suggests that they are not grounded in fact.

Anderson (1945) working at Stanford University used observers in elementary schools to note the characteristics of teachers and the response of children. Authoritarian teachers tended to produce bossy behaviour among the children, while teachers who adopted a friendly style seemed to produce co-operative relations among the children. Staines (1958) observing and testing in English primary schools found that teachers tended to emphasize certain characteristics of children in their class and that this affected the self-picture of the children. Thus a teacher who laid stress on the consequences of failure and the need for passing examinations seemed to produce insecurity among the children. Their self-picture was undermined. Staines also reports that a teacher could act out a part to produce changes in self-picture among the children. Intentionally or not teachers are important agents, significant others in the interaction through which children learn a picture of their self.

The ability of teachers to control the interaction in the classroom and to influence the way children see themselves and their world makes it important to know how teachers judge children, particularly compared with parents. McIntyre, Morrison and Sutherland (1966) have shown how teachers categorize middle and working class children differently. Middle class children work well and so are evaluated according to their behaviour. But working class children, mostly resistant to discipline, are easier to categorize according to their performance at work. Hallworth (1962) detected three clusters of attributes used by teachers to rate pupils. The first was attainment, the second was classroom behaviour particularly in relation to the teacher and the third the ability to get on well with others. Barker Lunn (1970) found that teachers got more pleasure from teaching bright children and girls, who seemed more amenable than boys. Girls may give teachers a greater sense of achieving the moral and social as well as intellectual objectives that are deemed important. Cohen and Cohen (1970) found that primary school teachers stressed more general social traits such as politeness and reliability. Taylor (1968) found that infant school teachers felt tension because they thought parents held views very different from their own.

Children socialize the teachers
Most research has concentrated on the influence of teachers on children. But as in the family, the socialization that takes place in the school affects all parties. Student teachers will appreciate that children often give them the necessary clues to classroom procedures. Teachers and pupils bring to the school their own stocks of knowledge and their own ways of interpreting the world. With young children the flow of influence is liable to be one way. But older children are liable to reject openly or covertly the views of the teacher or see these as irrelevant. Geer (1968) has argued that this results in bargaining until a compromise is reached. Similarly Werthman (1963) examining the behaviour of delinquent gang members has shown how they respond to teachers in the classroom according to rules that they have worked out in advance. The trouble they cause is related to the degree to which teachers work within these rules.

The author (1971) was able to detect compromises between third and fourth form pupils in secondary modern schools and their teachers over standards of work and of behaviour. This negotiation was never in the open but the result of cues which teacher and pupils presented and which were interpreted to give each party a bearable time in the classroom. This view of pupil-teacher interaction as negotiation includes the socialization of the teacher. He learns to limit his ambitions in the classroom. New teachers, especially if they are students, arrive therefore in a situation which has been negotiated in advance, in which unwritten but binding rules exist, but which they have no way of knowing. Inevitably these rules are violated, often leading to trouble. The process of re-negotiation may take longer than is available on a short teaching practice and if the new teacher is not sensitized in advance to the need to establish new limits, or detect and reinforce old ones, disorder may result.

This view of the classroom situation inevitably raises the question of the way children look at the teaching role. It has already been stressed that children continually evaluate the performance of teachers, as well as manipulating the impression they give to them. But the basis of this evaluation may be very different from that of the teachers. Thus Taylor (1962) found that among both primary and secondary children, teachers were judged primarily by their ability to instruct efficiently rather than their personal qualities. Teachers may see themselves as progressive, friendly, and concerned with all aspects of the childs education, but the child has a clear picture of the good teacher. Michael *et al.* (1951), Allen (1961) and Taylor (1962) confirm that children expected discipline with fairness, instruction with expectation and cheerfulness with personal interest. School is a fact of life to children. It's there whether they like it or not. The Schools Council Enquiry Number One (1968) confirms this discrepancy between the views of teachers and children. Teachers rank vocational preparation low as a priority and moral education high. Children wanted the teacher to give them the skills to get a job and gave a lower priority to matters of character and behaviour.

In some classrooms there may be a conflict of views on what should be happening. This is clearest among older children. First they are looking for tangible help in getting the skills that they, and their parents, see as the main purpose of schooling. But the adolescent is also supported against many of the values which teachers are trying to transmit, through their peers and the mass media outside the school. Thus Sugarman (1970) drawing on his research among boys in London secondary schools has concluded that the values held are related both to achievement in school and conduct as rated by teachers. Those who gave little heed to the future adopted a passive view of their own place in the world and had low personal ambitions tended to be under-achievers and to be rated as poor in conduct within school. Orientation to the future, belief in mastering the world and individualism tended to go with high achievement and good conduct ratings. Sugarman argues that these values typify the middle class and therefore teachers. Those who hold working class values are handicapped in this climate at school.

The possible tragedy for the teacher can be seen in Jackson and Belford (1965 and 1967), discussing the joys of teaching among a sample of American elementary school teachers judged as among the best by supervisors. Joy was obtained from close contact with the children, from their looks and expression of pleasure. What mattered to exceptional teachers was not the definition and attainment of educational objectives over a period of time, but subjective and immediate feelings of success. But these are liable to be just the feelings that are hurt if the children reject what the teacher is doing. Taylor (1970) examining how teachers plan their courses also suggests that teachers are little concerned with systematically working out objectives and strategies for achieving them, and are more involved in immediate classroom issues. The perspectives that teachers bring into the classroom may revolve around morals, behaviour, co-operation and the achievement of short range goals. But the children may see things very differently and act to attain different goals. Negotiation is inevitable therefore even in the most progressive and enlightened classrooms. But in most teaching situations achievement, however short-range, is the measure used by the teacher for his own success as well as that of the children. He wants them to learn something and his satisfaction is in at least seeming to achieve this. But this makes the teacher vulnerable. The children can easily reward and punish him.

Holt (1969) maintains that children in school respond to the pressures exerted on them in such a way as to frustrate education. Some of these ploys are:

(a) Looking attentive rather than actually attending. At its worst this can be seen in the glazed but open eyes concealing a sleeping mind. Younger children will crease their brows, look thoughtful, scratch their heads and show every sign of trying, when they have frequently given up long ago.

(b) Acting docile. Children in school are rarely in a position to express actively their hostility to what is going on. An easy way out of frustration is to act in a docile way to avoid punishment. At its worst this can be seen in the child who has opted out. He is no trouble but he is wasting his and everybody else's time. Wickman (1928) in America and Gabriel (1957) in England have shown that such children are rarely a major concern of teachers, even though this behaviour may be a symptom of genuine disturbance.

(c) Playing the answer game. Young children are particularly good at giving the right answer without understanding the question. This is made easy for them by the tendency of teachers to give clues to the right answer. The teacher needs the satisfaction of seeming to succeed and ensures that the children give him tokens of this success.

(d) If all else fails, act stupid. This is the extreme way out for the child who not only gets the wrong answer, but experiences a succession of failures. At its worst it is a means of avoiding further humiliation. More commonly it is a way of opting out of the pressure to learn. It teaches the teacher to lay off.

This rather depressing picture of gamesmanship in the classroom is, to Holt, completed by the teacher acting as God, all-knowing and all-mighty. But children as well as teachers have written the rules of the game. In the classroom Barnes *et al.* (1969) have used a similar perspective to show that children play the game that the teacher wants them to play. They give the answers that the teacher wants, or he interprets them to mean what he wants. In this way the teacher keeps control over the content and direction of the lesson, but he has learned the limits within which he can operate from the children. He ensures that it is his version, his definition that is passed across. But the children teach him to accept that they can not be pushed too far too fast.

It has to be noted that this description of classroom interaction can be interpreted in contrasting ways. Some will see it as indoctrination through which teachers control children and try to determine their self-image and view of the world. But others could argue that teachers would not be in front of the class if their knowledge was not superior to that of children and that education can involve some negotiation, but ultimately, if the children are to learn anything, they have to be the subordinate party, whether faced with teachers, books, mass media, parents, employers or any other socializing agencies. The available evidence can be used to illustrate both views.

The children socialize one another
In this account of the school there has been one missing perspective. Most of the research starts from a teacher's view. But the crucial element in socialization is the way the learner sees things. This is difficult to investigate, but would probably show that children learn much from one another. Precker (1952) and Byrne (1961) indicate that friendships are usually formed between children who share similar values and attitudes. Barker Lunn (1970) has shown that children pick their friends from similar ability bands more frequently in streamed than unstreamed schools, but in both the tendency is to form groups of similar ability. The effect of friendship groups may be rather to reinforce existing characteristics than to promote new ones.

However, friendships and the direct influence involved may be of little importance compared with the concentration of many children at high density in classroom and school. Wolfson and Jackson (1969) report two intensive observational studies of nursery school children with an interval of six months between. They describe a child's life as full of constraints and frustrations through clashing with the desires of other children. Life was a string of minor mishaps. Some experienced as many as 30 such constraints on their actions every hour. Furthermore, children prone to mishap and frustration in the first study remained prone in the second. Children seemed to be consistently incapable of avoiding mishaps. Wolfson and Jackson conclude that extreme cases may suffer 16,000 such constraints before the end of nursery schooling. Translated across the whole school career, this gives a picture of the likely effect on children of ten or more years of compulsory schooling.

The evidence that now exists on the experience of children in school reinforces the need to view education as part of socialization, as interaction. Academic learning may be inseparable from social learning in the classroom. The experience of the child as he is assessed, constrained and labelled will influence not only how he sees himself as a person, but how he sees himself as a pupil.

This can be seen clearly in the research of Nash (1971), Barker Lunn (1970), Rosenthal and Jacobson (1968), Staines (1958), Werthman (1963) and Wolfson and Jackson (1969). All contain indications that children assess themselves on evidence provided by teachers. But Nash (1971), particularly, also shows that teachers and children in a classroom share assessments of the ability of those involved. Each child seems to know how others assess him and seems capable of accurately assessing the ability of others. This is why the amount of time spent in classrooms is important, particularly in the primary school with one teacher most of the time. Some children may be continually reinforced in their successful self-image by the recognition of their prowess by those around them But others may be continually reminded of their failure. There is little direct evidence showing how this occurs or how powerful it is. But all the evidence above suggests that a clue to under-, and indeed, over-achievement may lie in the quality of the interaction that occurs between children in classrooms and between the individual children and the teachers.

CHAPTER SIX

From family to school

SMELSER (1969) has argued that the change from a traditional family structure to the modern pattern occurred in the first decades of the Nineteenth Century. As work was separated from the home, as the hours of work of children were regulated, as industrial trade cycles replaced the agricultural way of life, supports for the family were organized. The school can be seen as one of these supports. Schooling is a universal feature of modernization.

The simultaneous organization of a new form of family life and of schooling must therefore be considered by reference to the characteristics of urban industrial society. But the experience of the child in the family and in the school is very different. This can be summarized as a difference between a small, intimate and emotionally involved group in the family and a school organization that has been shaped by legislation to cope with large numbers in set hours for limited purposes. Dreeben (1968) has maintained that what is learned in school is essentially the patterns of behaviour which are paramount in modern society. These can not be learned in the family. These patterns or norms are:

Independence

In school the child is taught that there are tasks that must be done systematically and independently. The child learns that he is expected to be self sufficient. It is only in school that this expectation is systematically organized and imposed. Individual achievement is continually being tested. One of the worst offences is to cheat and therefore violate the expectation that work will be done independently.

Achievement

In school the child is faced with standards he is expected to achieve. His performance is continually evaluated against that of other pupils. The children are expected to achieve, but if they fail they are not expected to complain. It is what you do rather than who you are that matters and in school the child soon learns whether he is a success or a failure through being assessed regularly. In the family, there is not only less stress on achievement, but the effects of failure are cushioned by allowances made by the parents.

Objective assessment

In school, children are judged according to objective criteria established either by reference to some universal standard, or by comparison with peers. The examination is the most obvious example. In this way children are categorized. In the family they are always special cases, but in the school favouritism is taboo. Being fair to thirty, limits the allowances that can cushion the treatment of individuals.

Limited obligation

In school the child first comes across relationships in which the obligations between those involved are limited. They interact with many other children in school but may know very little about them. Often they meet them only as monitors, partners in work or as members of the same team. Similarly there are limits on the obligations towards the child that a teacher will accept. The child must learn to limit his demands. As he gets older the demands that he can make of others in the school are progressively limited. In the family the child can make sweeping demands on the parents and the parents usually accept these as legitimate. But the attention-seeker in school is rapidly discouraged by teacher and children.

Dreeben argues that only within the context of the school can these four qualities be learned. What is learned in school is essentially the patterns of behaviour that dominate adult life at work, and in the other large organizations that typify modern societies. The socialization that takes place in the family is essential for the physical and emotional wellbeing of the child. In small-scale, structurally simple societies socialization within the extended family prepared children adequately for adult life. But our world of large organizations at work, in politics, religion, mass communications, social service, distribution and leisure call for a more bureaucratic, more contractual, more impersonal style of living. This style is mainly learned in school, not in the family. The family remains crucial in giving the child the basic responses, values and skills that enable him to interact with others. But beyond these there are more formal, impersonal skills that are learned in schools.

These differences between the family and the school as contexts for socialization can be summarized through a consideration of the freedom allowed the child and the adults to depart from exceptations that are defined in advance. Socialization is a two-way process in which both parties, not one only, are learning. In the school the rights and duties of teachers and children are clearly laid down, often by law. The 'contract' between them sets clear limits to the demands that they can make on each other. In the family there is more flexibility in the demands that can be made by parents and children on each other and the law is only concerned with extreme cases of neglect or cruelty. Technically, socialization in school is institution-alized to a greater degree than in the family. The peer group has even looser prescriptions for behaviour than the family. It is interesting to speculate on why formal agencies of socialization such as the school have been organized as family life has tended to become informal.

The contrasting environments of family and School

The concurrent trends towards smaller families within nuclear families and towards universal schooling backed by professional social services have altered the pattern of relations within which the child is socialized. A child today is likely to be in a family of four. The average household in 1970 consisted of 2·95 persons (Family Expenditure Survey, 1971). A half of all households are owner occupied and 30 per cent of dwellings are rented from local authorities (Social Trends, 1970). Contacts are liable to be kept up with grandparents and relatives. Young and Willmott (1960) and Rosser and Harris (1965) both stressed the strength of the mother-daughter link. But relatives are likely to visit or be visited, not lived with. The family life of children will incorporate a narrow range of relations. But the school offers a very different experience.

The narrow range of family contacts are probably more intense in their nature than those in more extended family groups. The number of children has probably been planned, even to their date of birth. The young child may be at the centre of intense parental ambitions focused on education, particularly among middle class and skilled working class groups (Floud *et al.* 1957, Martin 1954). Douglas (1964) has shown that parental attitudes are crucial in determining the achievement of children in school. Hopes and fears are now concentrated on few children in ambitious families. Douglas, Ross and Simpson (1968) and Jackson and Marsden (1962) both report that the successful children came from small families. This confirmed Nisbet (1953) and Fraser (1959) finding that not only school performance but measured intelligence was higher in smaller families. But the small family may not be a suitable environment for learning all the social skills that the young need.

The most imposing evidence for the importance of home environment has come from the research for the Plowden Report (1967). Here, 3,000 children in English primary schools were tested. The major finding was that the dominant factor behind attainment was parental attitudes. Home circumstances and the schooling received were relatively less important. Of these parental attitudes the most important were ambitions for the children, the level of literacy in the home and interest in the children's work in school. Parental attitudes were more important for boys than girls and for older children. A follow-up of these children four years later by Peaker (1971) stressed the importance of home experience even more strongly. Secondary schooling seemed to have little effect. The early years set the pattern and the most important aspect of this is the home background, particularly the level of literacy. The crucial influence of the attitudes and literacy of parents indicates the power exercised within the small intimate family group. The combination of intimacy, intensive interaction in a small group and behaviour adjusted to individual characteristics makes the modern family a potent learning context particularly when the child is first learning to talk.

The Plowden evidence and Peaker's follow-up tend to confirm that teachers play only a small part in determining the achievement of children. However, Peaker points to three reasons why this may be pessimistic. It is hard to actually measure the effects of teaching; the range between best and worst in teachers is small compared with parents; and as everyone goes to school it is part of the general background of studies trying to compare the effects of different schools. It could also be argued that however small the teachers' contribution, it is easier to improve than that of parents and hence should be a priority for action.

Peaker reinforces the conclusions of the Plowden Committee that the available research suggests a need for more nursery schooling. But below academic achievement the school is teaching a particular form of social behaviour. Socialization in school is carried out partly through the distribution of knowledge in the classroom. It is continued in the club, the gym and on the games field. But it is most clearly seen in the way schools are organized. It is the organization of children within routines governed by fine distinctions of time and space that gives the school its unique flavour as an influence over children and that illustrates most clearly the contrast with life in the family.

Jackson (1968) in his book 'Life in Classrooms' has stressed three aspects of this hidden curriculum.

1. Life in the classroom is life in a crowd. In this crowd the child experiences delay, denial, interruption and distraction. He is involved in a complicated organization to deal with the large numbers involved. The teacher is exhausted by rapidly switching attention from one child to another. Thirty or 40 children have to be kept in order, kept to time, motivated to do the right things and supplied with the appropriate materials. For the child the consequence of being one in a crowd suffering frustration is to learn patience.

2. Praise and reproof are public in the school. In contrast to the private, confidential evaluation in the family, the child has to bear public reward and punishment in the classroom. He also has to satisfy two audiences, teacher and his peers. The child is also expected to work for approval, not gain it by subterfuge. His behaviour as well as his academic performance is being judged. Children soon learn that those who behave well have an easy time. From this public evaluation children learn compliance, or at least how to appear to be complying. The games people play to deceive one another may be first learned in the primary school classroom.

3. Unequal power is a fact of life in the classroom. However hard teachers try to make classrooms warm and friendly places, their

relations with individual children are unequal. Compared with life in the family, life in classrooms consists of interactions with relative strangers who wield ultimate power. This power is used to enforce and teach punctuality, attentiveness, ready response to command and at least the appearance of agreement with them. Going to school is itself a constraint on the child's freedom. But in most cases, go they must. Once there they must learn that in some things obedience will be enforced. Once again, the only defence may be to accept their powerlessness and play along with the teacher. The school classroom therefore may be the area where children first learn resignation. The habits of docility and obedience may be 'good' preparation for life in other organizations to follow.

Jackson is arguing that schooling is indeed a preparation for life, but not in the usual sense in which this term is used. Beneath the curriculum that is ordinarily discussed lie a series of experiences that have been organized to produce the level of conformity which is the normal condition of living together.

Wolfson and Jackson's (1969) observational study of nursery schools reported earlier suggests not only that life in classrooms consists of continuous constraint, whether from peers or teachers, but that a major part of this constraint is exercised on a minority of the children. Schooling not only consists of positive and negative pressures, but the distribution is uneven. Holt (1971) and de-schoolers such as Illich (1971) are saying that this is anti-educational, harmful to the children. Certainly education can be a strain. Moore (1966) found that some 65 per cent of children were reluctant to go to school at some time during their first year in the infants. In a study by Tennant (1971) including a review of research on non-attendance, some 10 per cent were found to be absent from school, including some one to three per cent of truants. In some urban areas it is likely to be greater. Schooling involves constraint. The de-schooling debate is largely over the gains and losses that children and adults incur as a consequence.

Bridging home and school
The movement of the child from family into school at five years of age is a form of social weaning. New ways of behaving, new forms of authority and new methods of evaluation have to be learned quickly.

Backed by the evidence that this pre-school period is crucial for the later development of the child, policy has increasingly been directed at providing pre-school facilities, to prepare children gradually and to organize infant schooling to continue this gentle socialization into the ways of the school.

Facilities for the under fives
There are a number of local authority and voluntary facilities for the pre-school child. There are private child-minders, play groups and private nurseries registered under the Nurseries and Child Minders Regulations Act of 1948. There are day nurseries provided by local authorities. These were expanded between 1939 and 1945 to enable women to go out to work, but the number declined until the late 1960s. There are nursery classes in maintained primary schools, nursery schools and children under five in infant classes.

The estimates in the Plowden Report (1966) were that seven per cent of all children under five years were receiving some form of nursery or school provision. Palmer (1971), rightly stressing the difficulties of obtaining accurate figures, suggests that 11 per cent were obtaining some pre-school education. However, Palmer has calculated that 21 per cent of children aged four were getting some form of nursery experience. The distribution of these facilities was uneven. The highest percentage receiving nursery-type education was among professional people and the next highest among unskilled workers.

The importance of this private and public provision is not that it gives children a lasting academic advantage. The follow-up studies to investigate this can not control all the factors that effect academic performance over the years, but Douglas and Ross (1964) report that the performance of children who had been through nursery schools was above average at eight years, average by 11 and below average by 15. The differences were however very small at each age. The great advantage is probably to prepare children for full time schooling, particularly to adjust them gently to being with other children in an organised and orderly situation. It helps them to adjust to adults who have charge of them but are strangers, and to other children who are met only within this controlled environment.

The Plowden Committee recommended that nursery schooling on

part-time basis should be made available for 35 per cent of three- to four-year-olds and for 75 per cent of four- to five-year-olds. A further 15 per cent of both groups should be able to attend full-time. Thus it was recommended that only a small minority would not have some form of nursery schooling. All the nursery groups were to be under the supervision of a qualified teacher with two year trained nursery assistants, in the ratio of one per ten children, doing the day to day work.

Starting school
It is now recognized that children entering the infant school are liable to be under stress as they leave the security of home for the bustle of up to 40 other children. The National Survey for the Plowden Report (1966) found that 45 per cent of children in their first term showed signs of tiredness towards the end of the school day. It is catering for these individual problems amid a large group, while simultaneously preparing children for life in school, that makes the infant teacher the foundation stone of the school system.

It is in the light of the transition from the warm, tailor-made environment of the family to the primary classroom with its order, stress on achievement and standards adjusted to group not individual that the organization of the infant school in general, and the reception class in particular, has to be viewed. A proportion of new children enter the reception class each term so that an experienced group can absorb the new entry. Admissions are staggered so that only a few new children come each day at the start of the term. Infant schools are allowed to work a shorter school day than that for the eight-year-olds and over. New infant schools are built with quiet areas where children can rest quietly away from the bustle.

It is in the organization of the infant school that the gradual socialization of children into life in schools can be seen best. Vertical grouping enables the new entrant to learn from others who have been in the school for a year or two. Such groups not only help the young however. They also take the strain off the older children who are finding difficulty in reading and other work as they can talk with the younger ones in the group without fear of being shown up as a failure. Above all vertical grouping is a half way stage between the situation in home and school. This is why the alternative name of family grouping is so significant. From the school's point of view it eases the problems of the new intake as children can be allocated to a number of classes rather than all to one. But it also brings more teachers into contact with fewer new children as well as using experienced children to help the novices.

The first few weeks of the child in school are also frequently adjusted by the teachers to limit stress. Many schools welcome parents and their children for visits before the day when the child is due to start. Palmer (1971) reports experiments in half-time schooling for rising-fives. Mothers are encouraged to bring their children, to come into the school and to call early if the child is showing signs of being very tired by the end of the school day. Some schools encourage parents to help in the classroom and around the school. Practice varies widely, but the trend is towards closer ties with parents of these younger children to make the transition gradual.

The National Survey for the Plowden Report (1966) found that over a third of all parents had not seen the head before their children started at the school. About two thirds of the schools in the sample had organized opportunities for parents to visit and talk over the work of the school and their child. However, the total number of meetings arranged declined as the proportion of semi-skilled and unskilled parents rose. Those schools with the highest proportion of professional parents arranged the most meetings at times when fathers could visit the school. Manual workers were less likely to visit the school. Similarly Jones (1966) found working class children less prepared for school than those from the middle class. Once again the picture that emerges is of handicap for the children of semi-skilled and unskilled workers. Unlike the children of white collar and skilled manual workers they had not the backing of parent-teacher co-operation. Disadvantages in the home were being re-inforced by lack of knowledge of the work of the schools. The opportunities to use the schools to advantage was greater for the parents of those children who probably needed little support and who had already been adequately prepared for school in home, play group and nursery class.

It would be wrong however to exaggerate lack of interest in

education among working class parents. Chazan, Laing and Jackson (1971) found that even among parents of deprived children 65 per cent would have liked nursery schooling, 95 per cent had visited the infant school to which their child was to go and only three of the mothers of the 61 children had not discussed the prospective school with their child.

Obviously not all teachers encourage a high degree of parental participation. Goodacre (1968) found that while some teachers encouraged parents to come to the school and show interest in the work of the school, others only wanted the parents to support their work through encouraging the child. Evidence in the Plowden Report (1966) showed that while most parents were satisfied with the arrangements for visiting schools, half would like to have known more about the progress of their children and a third thought that teachers should have asked them more about their children. Parents seemed to be aware of the importance of their own part in the education of their children and the need to align this effort to that of the teachers. What seemed to be missing was the organization to enable them to make this contribution.

The most significant advance in creating parent-school contacts where most needed may be the Educational Priority Areas research which was aimed to link the schools with the community in deprived areas of large conurbations. Midwinter (1970) working in the Liverpool area sees the Community School not as merely open to parents but as a way towards community regeneration. The primary schools are seen as the start of an education for children who will grow up motivated and equipped to tackle the social problems in the area. The curriculum has been based on studies of the community. As they are seen as likely to grow up and live in the priority area or in redevelopment estates, a thorough knowledge of the locale is seen as the basis for the work of the school.

This approach can be criticised as robbing the children of the opportunities that an education focused on the wide and more promising world elsewhere might bring. But it can be defended as realistic whereas the wider horizons view is both romantic and frustrating. The dispute illustrates the difficulty of viewing schooling without relating it to its social context. Conventional schooling may serve to bring home to the child that he is culturally deprived. It may succeed in giving the child the education that brings a good job, but this may be paid for by the child in alienation from his parents and friends. Alternatively the views typified by Bernstein (1970) that the social experience of the child should be reflected back to him as valid could merely confirm a child in his deprivation. The solution may be beyond the school in the province of social, not just educational, policy.

CHAPTER SEVEN

The gross material differences

STUDIES OF POVERTY have been prominent in the history of British social science. Rowntree (1901) and Booth (1902) have left a picture of the poor at the turn of the century in London and York. Rowntree (1941) and Rowntree and Lavers (1951) have provided comparisons of the impact and causes of poverty in York across half a century. By 1950 fuller employment, increases in real wages, smaller family size, improved social services and growing opportunities for women to work had reduced the incidence of poverty among families with young children. However, Abel Smith and Townsend (1965), re-applying the subsistence standard used by Rowntree and Lavers have shown that between 1953 and 1960 the proportion of the population in poverty actually increased. Across the same period Westergaard and Little (1970) showed that there had been little change in social inequality in access to selective secondary schooling.

Income, housing, access to social services, health and a decent environment set limits on the socialization of children. However, because there is little point in continually showing that poverty and inequality exist, attention is often concentrated on more subtle differences. These will be considered in Chapter eight. The danger in probing into complicated matters of motivation, the distribution of knowledge and linguistic codes is that the underlying inequality and squalor are overlooked. Yet inequality is finally a matter of money, housing and health. No enlightened programme of education can replace an attack on poverty and its attendant degradation.

Income

At a time when over half the households in Britain have a car and a quarter have central heating it is salutary to note that in 1969 one adult worker in 12, nearly a million in all, was earning less than £15 per week and that a quarter of these were taking home under £10 per week (Department of Employment and Productivity, 1969). By

1972 a disturbing pattern was developing. Inflation was accompanied by some trade unions forcing up wages while employers compensated on costs by paring down their personnel. Inflation and affluence on one side seemed to be increasingly accompanied by higher unemployment and very low wages on the other.

Abel Smith and Townsend (1965) found that 18 per cent of households and 14 per cent of the population, some 7,500,000 persons, were living below the best living standard provided on National Assistance. 4·7 per cent of households and 3·8 per cent of the population, some 2,000,000 persons, were receiving less than the basic National Assistance scale. About 30 per cent of the persons in these low income households, 2,500,000 in all, were children. Thus nearly one in five of all children were living in conditions of hardship. About five per cent of all children in the United Kingdom, 650,000 in all, were in households with incomes below the basic assistance scale.

Abel Smith and Townsend, following Rowntree and Lavers, expected most poverty to be found among the old. The extent of child poverty came as a surprise. A quarter of all these poor households contained six or more persons. Large families not only seemed to be still a cause of poverty but Abel Smith and Townsend found that the proportion of such large families among the poor households had increased from 11 to 25 per cent between 1953 and 1960. This suggests that the tendency for unskilled workers to have large families on low income persists. There are also the families worried with unemployment. But these are also the families who do not get the advantages out of the social services and education. They are the group who remain outside the affluent society and for whom trends in education, employment and the distribution of the available national resources, suggests an increasingly grim picture. Poverty is a relative concept and this group are the losers.

In 1966 the government carried out its own poverty survey (Ministry of Social Security, 1967). About half a million families with 1,250,000 children had too little for their minimum needs. This survey confirmed that large families still tended to be poor. Two per cent of children within one or two child families, 11 per cent in five child families and 20 per cent in larger families were in poverty. These figures may mean an improvement or that the government was measuring against a poverty level that was less generous than that used by Abel Smith and Townsend. But the inability of these poor families to make full use of the available social services, including education, was confirmed. Those most in need are in the worst position to use the help available. Thus 115,000 families containing 422,000 children were eligible to receive National Assistance but were not doing so.

Another Ministry of Social Security study into the effects of the wage stop (1967) whereby benefits were limited to what would have been received had the man still been in work, gives a picture of life among the poor in the affluent society. It applies to the lowest paid as well as the unemployed. One third of the men were in good health. Half the families owed rent. Several found difficulty finding money for food on the last days before receiving benefit. Fresh meat was eaten at weekends only. It was difficult keeping the children in shoes. A quarter ran short of fuel in winter. Bedclothes were often in poor repair or non-existent. Lambert (1964) examining trends in nutrition between 1950 and 1960 found that the three or four child family was worse off financially and was eating less well at the end of this decade. The Ministry of Social Security (1967) described the state of the poor in their sample as one of unrelieved dreariness and of little hope of improvement.

Housing
Woolf (1967), working for the Government Social Survey, reports that in 1964, 39 per cent of all houses in England and Wales were built before 1919. Cullingworth (1967) found that 44 per cent of Scottish houses were also built before this time. The House Condition Survey for England and Wales (1968) estimated that 1,800,000 houses were unfit for habitation. Privately rented housing accounted for 60 per cent of this total, yet only 25 per cent of all housing was in this category. Thirty-three per cent of privately rented accommodation was unfit.

When the lack of amenities which make up the unfitness of these dwellings is considered, its importance for young children becomes apparent. Seventy-nine per cent did not have a hand-wash basin. Seventy-seven per cent lacked an internal water closet and 72 per cent a fixed bath. Obviously the inhabitants of these unfit houses, were also those with low incomes. It was also the large families that were likely to be affected. Inevitably this applied to overcrowding which was particularly severe in Greater London. The Plowden Report on Children and their Primary Schools (1966) commissioned a national survey of 3,000 parents. Only three per cent of social class 1 families were judged to have too few bedrooms, but this applied to 43 per cent of those in social class 5. Earlier Douglas and Blomfield (1958) found that in 1950 26 per cent of children were sharing their beds with brothers, sisters or adults.

Homelessness is also a problem largely confined to Greater London and Birmingham. Annual reports of the Ministry of Health and Social Security (Social Trends, 1970) show that at the end of 1967, over 2,000 families were in accommodation for homeless families in London, making up nearly half the national total. By 1969 this had risen to 3,000, two thirds of which contained three or more children. But there may have been other homeless families for whom there was no local authority accommodation. Before 1966 these families were often split up. The official policy is now to try to keep families together, although Harvey (1969) has argued that injustices remain.

On the brighter side, over a third of all housing has been built since 1945. The large family tends to get priority on local authority housing lists because of the points system. The privately rented sector is steadily diminishing, although it still includes most of the problems. Smaller family size means that fewer problems arise. But the poor still tend to have large families and local authority building is concentrated on two or three bedroomed houses. This is the root of the problem. The large houses tend to be old and owned privately. Supply and demand are not adjusted.

The growing stock of new buildings has one dark side. Jephcott (1971) estimates that in 1968 there were 300,000 local authority dwellings in flats of five storeys or over. In multi-storey flats in Glasgow, 27 per cent contained one or more children aged 0–15. Jephcott's conclusions confirmed that of Maizels (1961) from London that such flats were unsuitable for children. They were a strain on mothers and provided a very restricted environment for the children. This could be compensated by imaginative planning around the flats but inevitably children were more separated from their homes if they were allowed to play around the flats on the ground, or over-restricted if their parents were more anxious and tried to keep them indoors. Yet this Glasgow sample were still pleased they had moved. The new may have disadvantages, but it is better than the old. Indeed, the National Survey for the Plowden Report (1966) found that 11 per cent of families of unskilled workers had no play area for their children around their houses. The higher the social class the more children played in their own homes and gardens. The children of manual workers were more dependent on parks, playgrounds and streets. Yet 13 per cent were found to play in streets not specially designated as play areas. Lack of facilities in and around the home tend to coincide with a similar lack in the environment.

Differences between North and South
The most disturbing feature of the uneven increase in affluence is that it is distributed so unevenly. The next two chapters will deal primarily with social class differences. But the distribution of opportunities and facilities for a decent life are also greater in the South than in the North of England. This is partially because the proportion of manual to non-manual workers is greater in the North and that lower wage industries such as steel, mining, shipbuilding and heavy engineering are concentrated there. It is also aggravated by the tendency for labour to move South in search of employment, thus reducing the need for any rapid replacement of amenities in the North.

Taylor and Ayres (1969) have collected together statistics on North-South differences to give a remarkable picture, aptly titled *Born and Bred Unequal*. There is no attempt in this book to sort out causes and effects. The economic and social factors cluster together, mutually reinforcing to produce contrasting regional environments. The basic economic factor is that the South East and West Midlands have the highest level of incomes and the Northern region the lowest.

The list of associated differences is long. A line from the Wash to the Bristol Channel has the highest incidence of death rates for bronchitis to the north, the lowest to the south. Similarly, with allowances for urban-rural differences this line has highest rates for still births, neo-natal and post neo-natal deaths to the north and the highest rates for industrial injuries. But the size of doctors' lists is lowest to the south of this line. The House Conditions Survey (1967) showed that 42 per cent of unfit houses were in the Northern economic planning regions. The Sample Census (1966) also confirms that absence of a fixed bath and inside water closet is more frequent in the North than the South.

When features of local conditions are combined, the picture is one of gross inequality. Crawford, Gardner and Morris (1968), working from the 1961 census using such indices as overcrowding, unemployment and the proportion in low income employment to give a measure of social factors found that northern county boroughs came out worst. It is the way poor conditions cluster together and the concentration of low income housing in such areas that is the root of the problem. In this study latitude and softer water also seem to have contributed to the higher incidence of bronchitis and cardiovascular disease in the North.

Another index of the inequality of North and South is in the ability of local authorities to raise money from rates. The product of a penny rate which is an index of the income available for paying for local services again shows that the poorest areas are the Northern industrial towns, the richest in the South East. The areas with the greatest need have the least resources. The consequences of this inequality is marked in all parts of the education system. The age of school buildings, expenditure on schools, length of school life, going on to higher education and the existence of independent schools have different patterns in North and South. Unfortunately the underlying economic factors give little hope of any rapid equalization and the trend has been for the ambitious to migrate from the North in search of better opportunities elsewhere. The major brake on this migration is probably the price and shortage of houses in the South East. There is no sign that policies aimed at economic revival in the North are working. Inequality at all ages is likely to remain. But because education is the most costly local authority service the impact is likely to be felt there most severely. The most depressing figures presented by Taylor and Ayres show gross inequalities in the money available per child in school. Furthermore, they stress that if the number staying on in school and going on to university did increase in the North the local authorities would approach insolvency.

Byrne and Williamson (1972) have shown that rich local authorities with a low proportion of poorer people tend to devote a higher proportion of their income to secondary schooling than authorities with a high proportion of lower social class groups. The richer authorities tend to support an élitist school system. The poorer authorities give higher priority to primary schooling and hence to a more egalitarian system. The result may be to give further support to inequality throughout the country and to North-South differences in particular.

Children in the welfare state
While the spotlight in history has usually been on the conditions of men, the most fortunate improvements in the human condition have probably come among women and children. Yet there will always be a number of children in need and as standards of welfare rise, always a number who do not seem to be receiving adequate help. Packman and Power (1968), in a report prepared for the Seebohm Committee on Local Authority and Allied Personal Social Services (1968), estimate that one in ten children are in need of help, but only half of these are receiving it. One in 12 children was physically handicapped, one in 11 mentally handicapped and one in 17 socially handicapped.

Physical, mental and social handicaps obviously overlap. Packman and Power suggest that the core of this group were to be found among the families in poverty indentified in the poverty survey of the Ministry of Social Security reported in 1967. Problems do not occur in isolation. Philp (1963) investigating 129 families being helped by Family Service Units, reports that 37 per cent had one or both parents in poor general health and 87 per cent in poor mental health, including ten per cent with psychotic reactions and 63 per cent with personality disorders.

Material disadvantages are made worse by the greater number of children in manual workers' homes. This applies particularly to the unskilled working class. This combination of large families and small incomes has proved to be the major problem facing the social services, including education in the welfare state. Inevitably the quality of maternal care is affected. Thus Douglas and Blomfield (1958) calculated that 62 per cent of mothers in the unskilled manual group were in the worst of three categories, best, intermediate and worst of standards of child care. But these were also the mothers who made the least use of child welfare centres. These mothers were carrying the heaviest burden with the least support. Survival seems itself to have been a triumph.

The triumph of survival applies also to unsupported mothers. Holman (1972) studied 95 women, mostly unmarried mothers. The results confirm those of Marsden (1968), Wimperis (1960) and Wynn (1964) that this group suffer from low income, poor accommodation and inadequate day care for their children. Poverty dominated their lives. One third had incomes below the level of the Ministry of Social Security supplementary allowance. Over half had an income below £10 per week. Typically they lived in privately rented accommodation giving least security and worst conditions. This is not a small problem. In 1965 there were 66,249 illegitimate births out of 862,725 (Registrar-General, 1967). The Seebohm Report estimated that there were 672,000 illegitimate children and 1,390,000 in families broken by death, divorce or separation.

Illegitimate children are continuously disadvantaged. Crellin, Kellmer Pringle and West (1972) in a follow-up study from 1958 to 1965 have shown that compared with legitimate children the illegitimate have higher mortality rates, and by the age of seven were judged by teachers as less able and were more prone to maladjustment. As Pond and Arie (1971) calculate that children in care or in schools for the maladjusted cost £500 per year, support for mothers may not only be humane but could save money. The Seebohm Committee has recommended that social services for children should be integrated with other services, particularly those for the mother. The work of children's departments was to become part of the new comprehensive social service departments. Part of the work was to be to find those families who made no use of infant welfare clinics. Help is needed early, but often comes too late, creating more long term problems. Even when available it may not be used. Douglas and Blomfield (1958) found that 28 per cent of mothers never used child welfare clinics.

The tendency for handicaps to overlap follows from this association of poor material background, reinforcing disadvantages and failure to use available help. Rutter, Tizard and Whitmore (1970) investigating children on the Isle of Wight found that one child in six in the middle years of schooling had a chronic or recurrent handicap. Ninety per cent of the intellectually retarded had other handicaps, one third of them being physical. These children often came from larger and poorer families. Although services for the handicapped were judged to be good by comparison with the rest of the UK they were still inadequate.

This concentration of problems among a group of families with low incomes, poor health and bad housing lies under many of the problems that occur within the schools. Behind the sophisticated analyses of educational under-achievement and inequality are gross material factors which may make remedial action on the organization of schooling a waste of time. Symptoms make interesting material for research but their treatment may leave the problem untouched. The pen is not necessarily mightier than the bulldozer.

CHAPTER EIGHT

Social class differences in education

(a) In education

IN THE NEXT two chapters the focus will be on social class differences in socialization. In this chapter the emphasis will be on the extent of these differences. In Chapter nine the factors that lie underneath these differences will be investigated. The accumulation of evidence on inequality of educational opportunity has been a major concern of social scientists. The acceptance of this evidence has probably been the major political triumph of sociology in Britain. Radicals and Conservatives accept the description even though they argue over the reasons for the inequality. Since the Early Leaving Report (1954) official publications on education have been liable to include a section on inequality of opportunity and the major reports have been based on research by social scientists.

Up to 1960 priority in research had been given to establishing that there were social class differences in educational opportunity and in the early experience of the children in the family. In the next decade the attention within the Sociology of Education switched to the school and the effects of streaming and selection. At the same time, sociologists became more interested in the way in which differences in motivation and achievement were learned. This interest has continued, concentrating particularly on the part played by language in socialization. Meanwhile clues to inequality are being sought in the school curriculum and in classroom interaction. The sequence has been therefore to establish first that the problem existed and then to ask the question 'how does it come about?'

As early as 1926, Lindsay (1926) had shown that working class children were underrepresented in the existing secondary schools. In 1938 Gray and Moshinsky (1938) published two studies which used intelligence tests to measure ability and then investigated what proportion of the highly intelligent children received secondary education. Out of their sample of 10,000 children of IQ of over 130 points, all those with professional fathers were in secondary schools, 50 per cent of those with clerical fathers, 30 per cent of those with skilled manual fathers and only 20 per cent of those with unskilled manual fathers.

By the time conditions had returned to normal after 1945 it was hoped that the 1944 Act giving secondary education for all would rapidly bring with it equal opportunity. The studies by Floud, Halsey and Martin (1956) did indeed show that working class children were entering the secondary grammar schools in numbers proportional to their performance on the selection tests. But it was also apparent that working class children had a smaller chance of getting a grammar school education than children from the middle class.

The Early Leaving Report (1954) showed that even when the working class child entered the grammar school he was more likely to leave before taking 'O' level than his middle class peer. This official report placed the causes of this drop-out in the home and community life of the working class pupils. This relationship and the consequently disappointing results of secondary education for all was confirmed by Fraser (1959) using evidence collected in Scotland. Confirmation of high wastage among working class pupils came in the Crowther report (1959) and the Robbins report (1963). Further evidence of this wastage appeared by the publication by Douglas (1964) and Douglas and Ross (1965) of the experience of the sample followed up from birth through primary and secondary schools. It has been impossible to establish an accurate trend across this period. But this difficulty was itself significant. Secondary education for all had not been universally beneficial. Westergaard and Little (1970), analysing the evidence from surveys in the 1950's, concluded that social inequality had only been slightly reduced, and this was a gradual reduction, not the result of post-1944 developments.

The most obvious point of attack for both reformers and researchers in the light of this accumulating evidence was the selection tests for secondary schooling. The debate over the intelligence test and the degree to which it measures inherited characteristics as distinct from learned abilities has continued to the present. The studies above had shown that working class children had a lower measured intelligence than those from the middle class.

But there is no agreement on what intelligence tests measure, because there is no agreement over the definition of intelligence.

There have been three major attempts to increase the achievement of working class children. The abolition of selection for secondary schools, de-streaming and the introduction of varieties of comprehensive schooling. The 11+ examination using objective tests was a symptom of selective secondary schooling and its abolition in some areas was more a gesture of reform than a solution to inequality of opportunity. Indeed, the intelligence test, having been designed to be objective, may have been unfair to working class children but may nevertheless have been more fair than any other way of selecting. Floud and Halsey (1957) found that giving up such tests in South-West Hertfordshire actually reduced the chance of working class children obtaining a place in the grammar schools.

The evidence of Douglas (1964) that the advantage of the middle class child was apparent in the primary schools and that the gap between him and his working class peer tended to widen with the years seemed to confirm the conclusions of anti-streamers such as Daniels (1959) that streaming was responsible for the widening gap. But a replication of this study by the Surrey Educational Research Association (1968) later came to opposing conclusions. Other studies such as Morris (1959) actually suggested that streaming was beneficial in such areas as learning to read. Yates and Pidgeon (1959) from the neutral position of the National Foundation for Educational Research warned that caution should be exercised in drawing conclusions from the available evidence. Indeed, the way this evidence was produced, publicized and used was highly selective, supporting a case, not investigating an issue (Shipman, 1972). In the early 1960s the campaign was at its height. The way had been cleared by the abolition of selective tests for secondary selection in many areas. But the large scale study for the NFER (Barker Lunn, 1970) avoided the dogmatic tone of the small scale studies. The crucial factor appeared to be the attitude of the teachers involved. They could make de-streaming work, but equally could frustrate it if they were not convinced of its value. The Plowden Report (1967) confirmed that the middle class child had an advantage over his working class opposite number and came out strongly for the un-streamed school. The next stage in the campaign to equalize opportunity in schooling was to reinforce the existing pressure for comprehensive secondary schools.

It is too early for reliable evidence to have been produced on the effects of spreading comprehensive schooling. As with the evidence on streaming there are lobbies for and against, producing conflicting evidence. There is less doubt about the spread of comprehensive schooling (Benn and Simon, 1970). But the comprehensive schools have tended to remain streamed and the next phase in the reform movement was to state that 'reorganization is not enough' and press for de-streaming in the secondary schools (Armstrong, 1969).

The success of the comprehensive school movement has also not been accompanied by any satisfaction that re-organization is producing social mixing. Holly (1965) and Ford (1969) have both found that friendships are still within different social class groups in streamed comprehensive schools. Fisher (1972) has however found that this does not apply when they are unstreamed. Tapper (1971) suggests that comprehensive schools are a step towards a meritocracy. They cream off a thicker layer and prepare more children for external examinations, but this only accentuates the feeling among those not selected that they have already lost and that school and future work will offer them little material reward.

The focus of attention of those interested in promoting more equality of opportunity in education has concentrated more on the curriculum and teaching styles as re-organization has failed to have a marked effect. The usual approach is to suggest that teachers promote a middle class culture in the schools and thus present working class children with the alternative of learning this new culture and rejecting that of their friends and families or rejecting the values, and the content, of schooling. This is the view adopted by Jackson and Marsden (1962) and Bernstein (1961 and 1970).

This view of the school classroom as the centre of a clash between two social class cultures underlies the work of Barnes (1969 and 1971) on the use of language in the classroom, of Lacey (1970) and Hargreaves (1967) on streaming, and of Young and others (1971) who see knowledge as packaged and distributed by the middle class for consumption by the working class. The difficulty in accepting this argument in any bar very general terms is first that the term social class is so crude. Sometimes it only seems to apply to the lower working class and the middle middle class. More dubiously it seems to be applied to that largest and confused section of the population embracing the skilled working class and the white collar workers. In this group where manual workers may have higher incomes than their white collar neighbours, where home and car ownership among both groups exceeds 50 per cent and where attitudes to schooling tend to be positive, it is difficult to see the validity of the culture clash hypothesis when argued in terms of middle and working class.

Witkin (1971) in a rare attempt to investigate the culture conflict hypothesis in the classroom found that it had to be rejected. Three thousand four hundred children in 36 schools were questioned on attitudes to lessons. Indeed, Witkin actually found that working class children were more positive towards school in general and English lessons in particular than children from the middle class. Witkin is not denying the importance of social class differences in schooling. He puts forward an alternative model, still based on social class differences but postulating that the school can influence the working class child more than a middle class child. The middle class child experiences similar expectations of his behaviour in school, home and community. Consequently he can view his life in school against his experience outside. This enables him to benefit from education, but frees him to disagree and oppose the values of the teachers. His experience outside the school fits him to be objective about life inside. The working class child does not have the home and community experience that facilitates a detached assessment and rejection of school values. He accepts and may enjoy schooling. But this lack of freedom to interpret what goes on in school simultaneously reduces his chance of using education effectively. In Witkin's terms the middle class child has an articulated social experience, but the experience of the working class child is non-articulated. This difference in articulation, not the existence of conflicting class cultures, may be the key to differing class experiences in school.

Witkin's choice of children's evaluation of English lessons is especially significant. The working class child would be expected to feel under attack here, a victim of alien values. But instead he seems to enjoy English better than his middle class peer. Witkin is showing that working class children can divorce academic problems from the rest of their experience in a way that is impossible for the middle class child who interprets academic life as an articulated part of his total experience.

This dispute is over the most appropriate model for explaining the social class differences in the benefits of schooling. It indicates the difficulty of defining terms like social class or social class values, the difficulty in collecting evidence that can illuminate the strengths and weaknesses of these conflicting models and the perils of assuming the apparently simple and obvious idea of a clash of culture in school. There is enough evidence to be sure that social class differences exist and affect children in school. But there is a lot of theory and little evidence about the way these differences actually take effect. The evidence that exists suggests that the original model of culture clash was too simple to account for the complex interaction that takes place within school, and between schooling and other socializing influences.

(b) *In the family*

There is not only a great variety of child-rearing practices among different societies. There are a range of diverse practices within contemporary Britain. Klein (1965), distinguishes a deprived group, a traditional and rough, traditional and respectable working class, middle and upper middle class with a number of sub-groups striving for higher social status. She then presents evidence on different practices within these groups across the spectrum from attitudes to conception, to discipline and to the child's future. Children born today in Britain may have very different experiences as they learn to become social.

The trend in the evidence presented so far suggests that social class differences appear very soon after birth. This has been confirmed in the longitudinal research project at the Centre for the Study of Human Development at the University of London, Institute of Education (Hindley, 1965). Hindley has reported that by using tests of both abilities and personality, the observation of play and the reports of those looking after the children, it is possible to detect social class differences in performance at three years. Between three years and five years, the IQ of children from higher social class groups rose. But the IQ scores of children in lower class social class groups fell. Among children who were equivalent at 18 months, the middle class children had gained on average, 17 IQ points by the age of five, while children of semi-skilled workers and unskilled workers lost ten points by the time they were five. This study was only of some 200 children, but the results were similar to others from parallel investigations in Stockholm and Brussels. They are also consistent with the findings of several American studies.

Confirmation of this early determination of ability has come from Sampson (1956) and Moore (1967 and 1968). Sampson found that the quality of the home life of the child seemed to be influencing the speech development of the child as early as 30 months. Moore established a relation between the provision of toys, books and their use at two-and-a-half years and reading ability at seven and intelligence quotient at eight. Most convincing of all, Davie, Butler and Goldstein (1972), studying nearly 16,000 children from birth to seven found that by the age of seven a wide gap had opened between children of middle class and semi- and unskilled working class parents. The former were 1·3 inches taller, better adjusted in school, superior in oral ability and only one in twelve was a poor reader compared with nearly half of the unskilled group.

Studies such as that by Newson and Newson (1963 and 1968) in Nottingham or by Douglas and Blomfield (1958) covering some 13,687 children distributed across the country are among many illustrating the remarkable differences in the way in which different social classes bring up their children. Children of manual workers, compared with their middle class peers, grow less tall, are more prone to illness and death, more likely to enter hospital, and more prone to get the infectious diseases of childhood. Below these differences lie low income, poor housing and unhealthy environment. As the children get older social class differences become very marked. Kellmer Pringle, Butler and Davie (1966) examining 11,000 seven-year-olds found that middle class groups already contained a higher proportion of the good readers and those good at arithmetic than the working class groups. But most of the children not living with both natural parents were in working class groups.

Social class differences appear in the most intimate sectors of family life. Newson and Newson (1963) found that in their

Nottingham sample practices changed between the five social classes studied. The higher up the social scale the less chance was there that the first birth would take place when the mother was twenty-one or younger. The lower down the social scale the shorter was the period of breast feeding, but the longer was the period during which bottle feeding continued. Working class children were more likely to be given a dummy and to be given it or the bottle if they would not sleep. Middle class children were put to bed earlier.

Some of these differences were obviously related to housing conditions and income. The higher up the social scale the more likely was the child to sleep in a room alone and to have an adequate diet. Similarly the greater participation of father in the bringing up of the middle class child was probably related to his hours and type of work. Similarly working class children were more likely to be smacked. But the other differences seemed to be reflections of different life styles. Thus the lower the place on the social scale the more frequently was genital play stopped, the less likely was the child to be told the facts of life or to see brothers and sisters naked as part of normal family life.

The pattern of these differences suggests that the material difficulties faced by working class families, particularly where father was an unskilled worker were aggravated by difficulties with children. Potty training was started later in working class homes and the chances of early success were less, particularly among this unskilled group. Newson and Newson (1968) found that this difference persisted when the children were four years old. The unskilled parents were still getting much more bed wetting. The children of the unskilled were also subject to more tantrums. Behaviour difficulties were added to material disadvantages. The Newsons concluded that there is first a manual, non-manual worker divide in child rearing patterns. The second rift is between the unskilled workers and the rest. This second division meant that life was particularly tough for the wife of the unskilled worker. Not only did she have to cope with poor material conditions, low income and bad health, but the children were more troublesome and the father less likely to help bring them up. As she was likely to have more children than wives in any other group she was the real loser in this recurrent pattern of a persisting submerged tenth.

It would be wrong however to see even the unskilled manual worker group as homogeneous. Klein (1965) using evidence from community studies distinguishes first a deprived, submerged group. At this level little real effort was made or was possible to bring up children systematically. Early indulgence was followed by neglect. Even the very young child seemed to be left to his own devices in a harsh world.

The remainder of the solid working class seems to divide conveniently into 'rough' and 'respectable'. The respectables rely on tradition to bring up their children. They have very clear ideas on child rearing which are obtained for the most part from their mothers. The result is a firm and very moral upbringing. The respectable, traditional working class family will often be very critical of the 'roughs' who make it hard for them to retain high standards. The children will tend to mix even though the parents remain separated. Even this crude categorization has probably been disturbed by the amount of rehousing which has taken place since 1950. Rehousing is itself disturbing to families but the net consequence appears to be to make family life as distinct from community life more important.

The most direct comparison between social classes has been made by Spinley (1954). In her book *The Deprived and the Privileged* she compares a sample of slum children with those who had been to public school. This book is based on the memories of those involved and may not be very reliable, but it is a direct comparison. The picture is of a public school sample brought up under consistent attempts to mould their characters. The carrots and the sticks that were used in this moulding were derived from a consistent picture of the future life of the child communicated to the children by the parents. The children in the slums, by contrast, enjoyed a very easy-going first year of life, but this ceased as soon as the next child arrived. They were now no longer a centre of attention and from that time grew up without any consistent affection or guidance.

These studies of social class differences in socialization are important for education because they suggest where the differences in the motivation and performance of children arise. So far however only social class differences in educational performance and similar differences in early family life have been described. These do little more than show that the problem exists. They do not show the process through which early experiences in the family influence performance later in school. The explanation of this connection is crucial if the consequent waste of talent is to be reduced. Thus there is now a need to shift the focus from the question 'what differences exist?' to the question 'how do these differences arise?' and the related and even more important question 'what is it in the lives of very young children and their relation to their parents that seems to determine their success within the school?'. The focus must shift therefore to examining motives. This means attention to the way in which motivation is communicated to young children. It also involves an examination of the school and the curriculum, and the part played by children in these, to see if schooling remedies or reinforces the different motives acquired in infancy.

CHAPTER NINE

The motives and means to achieve

IN MOVING ON to a consideration of the subtler factors determining motivation and achievement, the gross inequalities must not be forgotten. There is always the danger that too much energy will be devoted to researching into more and more obscure areas, to the neglect of the obvious and remediable. It is first necessary to correct any impression that the research which has been done into the factors affecting the motivation of children has produced results over which there is universal agreement. Knowing that there is a relation between social class and educational attainment does not explain how it came about. Usually cultural differences are assumed to be the link. But Byrne and Williamson (1972) have challenged this model and shown that other explanations based on the resources made available may be more powerful. Researchers are also dependent on answers to questions and there may be a serious gap between what has been said to have been done and what actually was done to the children. More serious, the available research gives us the detached investigator's view, not that of the individual actually involved. Behind the available evidence lie the rapid changes in child-rearing practices. If there was a simple relation between these practices and the personality of the child, we could expect alarming changes in the nature of our children. In reality, the changes that have taken place have occurred in the tip of the iceberg that truly represents the relationship between parents and children. Ideally, all the interrelated factors in family life should be studied simultaneously, not a study of one factor after another, extracted arbitrarily. But to set up such an investigation would destroy the family life being studied.

The definition of social class
Most studies use father's occupation as an index of social class. This is usually reliable as this index seems to relate highly to the

other important features of social class. The difficulty is that categories such as middle class or working class, while sufficient to demonstrate the differences of living patterns between them, conceal many variations within each. No single family within any social class level will correspond in all its features to the description attached to that social class.

One advance has been to define social classes by observing common features between social groups, rather than using a single, arbitrary index such as father's occupation. A common distinction is between the 'respectable' and 'rough' elements within the working class (Lupton and Mitchell, 1954, Stacey 1960). The separation of these two groups from a deprived group has already been described. Carter (1966) has distinguished the roughs from the solid working class and also distinguished a third, home-centred, aspiring type. This last category is useful in discussing education, for this group among the working class come nearest to the middle class in their use of the available facilities. Carter further subdivides this home-centred, aspiring group into the traditional respectables and the newly affluent.

Goldthorpe *et al.* (1969) suggest three categories of working class, proletarian, deferential and privatized. The privatized worker, usually found in the most modern types of industry, living on a suburban housing estate confines his activities very much within the family. He takes interest in his children's education and is very keen for them to do well.

Similar efforts have been made to discriminate between various middle class groups. Swift (1968) distinguishes homes where learning is valued for itself and education seen as intellectually liberating, from those homes where learning is valued for the job it will bring and education seen as socially liberating. Jackson and Marsden (1961) found a sunken middle class who made up a high proportion of the families of sixth formers in the grammar school they were investigating. The important point for the reader in all these classifications is that the researcher is forced either to use an arbitrary index and compress the persons studied into the categories so defined, or to detect actual groups and generalize from them. In either case there is distortion, and the reader needs to exercise caution in interpreting the results.

Implicit in the argument above has been the idea that practices by parents or teachers have to be related to the total environment from which they have been extracted by the researcher for them to have real meaning. But before considering further the evidence from sociology on the factors underlying educability, the possible part played by inheritance must be acknowledged. No lengthy treatment is possible here. The crucial point is that any model of intelligence is designed to facilitate research. The model is synthetic, not an actual description, just as social classes as used by sociologists are synthesized from observations of actual groups.

Most models usually assume some deep, innate area of intelligence which cannot be measured directly. Therefore we do not know how it is distributed between the various social classes. We may be all born equally intelligent, or we may be handicapped or favoured before birth. The most popular model is drawn from Hebb (1949) and Vernon (1969). This pictures an innate part, genetically determined, that is labelled intelligence A. Intelligence B is defined as that part that develops during socialization. It is the product of the interaction between intelligence A and the environment. Intelligence tests sample intelligence B. It is useful to label this intelligence C as it only coincides with B if the test used is perfectly reliable and valid, a most unlikely combination not approached so far, despite the investment in improving tests.

This model has the advantage of indicating that there is obviously such a thing as genetically determined intelligence. But it also has the advantage of indicating that the way that intelligence comes into play after birth is determined partly by what has been inherited, but also by what has been learned. In practice, parents and teachers concerned with the socialization of children might be best advised to leave the debate over the relative contribution of nature or nurture to the academically minded. As we can at present only alter the environment of children it is more profitable to concentrate on its improvement, rather than debating the extent to which it contributes. Any doubt about the futility of the debate can be settled by considering the furore following the publication of work by Jensen (1970) and Eysenck (1971) in Shipman (1972).

This issue is complicated by the relation between the distribution of intelligence, social class and family size. Children from large families tend, on average, to achieve less academically when compared with children from smaller families (Nisbet, 1953 and Fraser, 1959). But working class families tend to be larger than those of the middle class. Now the middle class child tends, on average, to have a higher measured intelligence than his working class peer. Could it be therefore that family size is the crucial factor in measured intelligence and from thence to achievement? We just don't know.

The attitudes of the parents

Probably the one finding on which all the research into educability has been unanimous is the importance of parental encouragement. Here at least is one finding which can apparently serve as a reliable basis for policy and action. The Plowden Committee (1967) found a high level of interest among parents in the education of their children, in all social classes. Predictably, interest was greater among middle class parents. This was most marked in the interest of the father. But the middle class parent also attended the school more frequently, talked with teachers and the heads, and helped their children with school work. Again the crude differences must not be neglected. The middle class homes had the facilities, particularly the books to help the children. Unfortunately, it was the children of unskilled workers who tended not to borrow books from the school, and these were the group who were not using the public libraries. Chazan, Laing and Jackson (1971) and Jones (1966) confirmed this and found that there was also a social class difference in reading to children.

Douglas (1964) found that middle class parents not only took more interest in their children's progress at school, but became more interested as their children grew older. These social class differences are based on a different knowledge of, and attitudes towards, the school system. The middle class parent knows how the system works, does not hesitate to ask teachers and heads about it, has often been through higher education and lives in a neighbourhood where education is treated very seriously. None of these factors applies as strongly among the working class. Among the unskilled manual workers particularly the world of the school may be alien. Teachers may be bracketed with policemen and other agents of an apparently oppressive group organized in a complex, aloof and hostile system.

The attitude of the parents seem to have a considerable effect on the actual performance of children in school. Douglas found not only that the highest average scores on the tests used were made by children whose parents showed the most interest in their education, but that this relation persists within each social class. The children of very interested parents within both middle and working class tend to achieve more. Furthermore, those children whose parents showed the high level of interest also increased their performance on attainment tests most between the ages of eight and eleven. The interest of the parents seemed to enable the child to pull ahead of the rest, whatever their initial starting ability. Even when the overlapping effects of standard of home, size of family and academic record in schooling are taken into consideration, parental interest still seems very influential.

Parental interest also seems to encourage the children to work well in school. Douglas showed that this was particularly the case among children of manual workers. Needless to say, these hard working children, with interested parents, were also those who were the least trouble to the teachers. In many ways therefore the interest of parents in the schooling of their children appears to be crucial. This is of practical importance. But it also reinforces the view that it is within the interaction in the family that the clues to later motivation and achievement lie.

Bloom (1964) reviewing the available evidence on the factors underlying the development of intelligence concluded that half the variation at the age of 17 was accounted for by the age of four. Furthermore, it was in these first four years that the cultural environment had its maximum effect. Hess and Shipman (1968) investigating the styles and strategies used by mothers in preparing their pre-school children for later learning found large social class differences. Middle class mothers controlled their children, conversed with them and initiated behaviour that helped them towards effective learning strategies. Working class parents seemed to be producing less effective, more passive attitudes towards new knowledge.

In Britain these contrasts in the styles used for raising children and the effects of social class differences in these styles on the ability of children to benefit from education have been developed in the work of Bernstein (1971). Here too the styles of control used by parents, particularly in the language used, is seen as the crucial element in early socialization. Kohn (1959) working in America takes a similar view. Miller (1971) investigating children in top primary classes in schools in Middlesex found that the children who got most out of their schooling came from families where independent thinking, curiosity and free discussion of problems were encouraged. These were more commonly found in middle class homes where the children could find reinforcement for the values of the school. Such conditions were less common in working class homes.

The conclusion of these and many other studies is that social class differences in the home, particularly the attitudes of parents towards education, are crucial in determining the achievement of children in school. But caution is needed over the interpretation of social class in this context. It is not an explanation of how differences come about. It frequently appears because many of the factors under investigation are unevenly distributed between social classes. It is these underlying factors that need to be uncovered and remedied.

Is the motive to achieve learned?
The importance of parental attitudes in promoting educational achievements suggests that motives to achieve have in some way been passed from parents to children. Obviously, parents who help their children, show an interest in their work and set standards are likely to promote good performance. But such early experiences may have a more profound, long-lasting effect. The motive to achieve, once learned, may persist as an influence on performance through life.

McClelland (1953) suggests that achievement motivation is learned through the manipulation of rewards and punishments during socialization. Evidence for the existence of such an acquired drive has come from history, experimental psychology and the study of the performance of children from different social groups. The experimental work suggests that middle class mothers seem to expect more of their children by way of independent action at an earlier age than do working class mothers. This experimental work has included studies depending on asking questions and on actually observing the behaviour of parents. The evidence from both suggests that some parents influence the personality of the children so that they seek high performance in all areas of their life. McClelland (1967) also suggests that people can actually be taught to achieve and be motivated.

There are a number of debatable retrospective studies supporting the idea that some groups seem to build an urge to achieve into their children. Before the theory of achievement motivation had been formulated Weber (1931) had traced a relationship between the Protestant ethic and the rise of capitalism. The Calvinist stress on personal austerity and hard work served to accumulate capital. The Calvinist belief in personal salvation supported a drive to prove eligibility for membership of God's elect. No confessional existed to relieve the individual of the burden of proving his worth on earth. Capitalism certainly seems to have advanced fastest and furthest in Protestant rather than Catholic countries. Similarly Merton (1938) suggests that scientific activity was similarly stimulated by Protestant beliefs.

Weber and Merton were both drawing parallels between two historical trends. They were not particularly concerned with the way children were socialized into religious beliefs. Similarly Bradburn and Berlew (1961) have attempted a direct historical investigation of the achievement motivation hypothesis. Coal output in England from the Sixteenth to the Nineteenth centuries was used as an index of economic growth. Achievement motivation was measured through content analysis of the work of a random selection of authors in six periods within the time under investigation. They concluded that rises in achievement motivation were followed 50 years later by rises in coal output. Industrial growth seems to have been affected by the earlier investments of men with an urge to achieve.

Strodtbeck (1962) investigating the family life of Italian and Jewish immigrant families in America has traced the higher per-formance of the children of the Jews when compared with the Italians to their experience when young in the family. The Jews stress the importance of education and intellectual attainment. They were ambitious for their children, compared with the Italians who were more pessimistic about the chances of their children getting on in the world. The Jews seemed to believe that their future depended upon their own efforts, while the Italians believed that their destiny was outside their control. Studies within Italian and Jewish families on the same social class levels did not reveal any differences in the stress placed on early independence. But Italian fathers tended to give more support to their sons than the Jewish fathers. Jewish sons particularly appear to have been forced to depend on their own efforts.

The relation between parental motivation and achievement and that learned by their children is obscure. Swift (1966) examining the relation between the 11+ performance of lower middle class children to their father's view of his prospects of promotion at work, found that the father's pessimism about his job prospects was likely to increase the child's chances of success in the selection examinations for secondary schooling. Argyle and Robinson (1962) using a sample of 500 teenagers in Britain found that where parents were hard working and successful and the children identified with them, a drive to achieve seems to have been learned. The middle class parent may press his children to succeed, especially where he feels he has failed. But the successful middle class parents also seem to build high aspirations into their children.

The best family environment for the child who is to be successful and ambitious is not necessarily a happy, tolerant and democratic one in which to grow up. Eidusen (1962) found that successful American scientists frequently had little contact with their fathers and grew up in families that were the opposite of the warm, cosy nest that is often idealized. Similarly Warner and Abegglen (1955) found that successful American businessmen remembered their fathers as being cold and detached, weak and unreliable, rather than the friendly, solid citizens that we usually hold up as models. What comes over clearly is that the family life of those who are taught to achieve is by no means a soft option (Musgrove, 1966). It is not only tough at the top, it is tough learning to want to be there.

There have been many attempts to investigate the relation between achievement motivation and academic attainment. Many questionnaires have been designed to measure achievement motivation, but even McClelland (1958) doubts if all these are actually measuring the same thing. Most of these investigations have been with students or older children. An exception is Bruckmann (1966) studying children in the third and fourth forms of three London primary schools. He found that there was a relation between achievement motivation and the stream in which the children were placed. However, when the intelligence of the children was taken into account the relation between achievement motivation and stream became minimal.

It is difficult to consider achievement motivation as anything but the consequence of an amalgam of values, such as planning for the future, a striving to control the world and a willingness to break free from intimate groups to press towards individual goals. But these values are obviously related to each other and to many other characteristics. Lavin (1965) reviewing ten American studies found that the results were inconsistent, only four giving significant associations between achievement motivation and attainment. Heckhausen (1967) citing 23 experiments reports that 16 found positive relationships between achievement motivation and academic performance. However, Hartley, Holt and Hogarth (1971), re-examining these studies, report that even taking a generous view, rather less than half really found such a positive relation and where this was found it was small. Achievement motivation does not seem to be a crucial isolable personality trait. What can only be said with confidence is that a positive attitude to learning is associated with a high level of achievement (Barker Lunn, 1972).

The part played by language
Socialization, always a two-way process, is a form of communication. A crucial part in understanding the process is therefore the examination of language. Two cautions are necessary in approaching the available research. First, there are fundamental differences in the approaches that have been made to the study of the development and use of languages. Secondly, the work connected with Bernstein in Britain which will be considered here is an evolving, not a finished theory. Bernstein (1971) maintains that the only paper of his worth reading is the next one to be written. Furthermore, the theory and the evidence that has been collected to verify it relates not to language alone, but to a theory of socialization.

The linguistic codes postulated by Bernstein, in their later versions (1971a), are important because they may lead to different perspectives of society and self. Elaborated codes allow the speaker to verbalize his subjective intentions. They involve complex planning. They arise where the intentions of other people can not be taken for granted and the speaker has to concentrate on the experience of others rather than himself. Restricted codes by contrast do not facilitate expression of subjective intentions. The pattern of the language is predictable. But a restricted code is not necessarily restricted in its vocabulary. It is neither jargon nor the speech of the inarticulate. Elaborated codes may only arise in situations where personal relations require that meanings have to be elaborated and made precise and explicit. Some working class children may not learn this type of code.

Bernstein (1971a and 1971b) develops a sophisticated theory of the relation between social class, language and socialization. He postulates two family types. In positional families there is a clear separation of roles and the decisions that any members can make are determined by reference to their positions as fathers, mothers and so on. Each person has a place and relations are rigidly defined. In these families the peer group plays a large part in socializing children either through close parental supervision among the middle class, or relatively free of parental interference among the working class. Personal families on the other hand work through psychological qualities rather than position. Socialization of the children is not left to peers but retained by the parents. Here it is differences between persons rather than positions that matters.

In person-centred families motives, intentions and meanings have to be verbally elaborated as personal interaction is subject to negotiation and qualification. Speech becomes a major vehicle for discipline and control. The members express motives as they relate to others and hence open themselves to verbal persuasion and control by others. In position-centred families control is exercised by reference to the clear-cut rights and responsibilities which go with positions. Reference is to what small boys should do because they are small boys. There is little verbal elaboration of the personal responsibilities of those involved. Learning about things and persons is reduced and there is little need for verbal elaboration.

Bernstein sees the possibility of restricted and elaborated language codes existing in both personal and positional families. However, positional families and restricted codes tend to go together and there is the suggestion that these occur among the working class. Personal families seem to be typically middle class and the children are consequently in a position to switch from one code to another. The implications of this divide for schooling are not confined to the difficulties of the child who can not accommodate to elaborated codes used by teachers, through experience that has been limited to restricted codes in the family, for these codes mirror different forms of socialization. The crucial area is therefore the modes of control to which the child has been accustomed and his ability to negotiate complicated personal relations and learning situations in schools.

As with other aspects of socialization the crucial period is again within the first years in the family. Robinson and Rackstraw (1967) asking mothers about the answers they would give to questions of the 'where from' and 'why' type from their five-year-old children, report that there was a clear social class division in the nature of the responses. The middle class mothers were more likely to give answers and to ensure that these were accurate. They used more analogies, more detailed answers and introduced less irrelevant detail. Working class mothers were more likely to repeat the question, were more evasive and more likely to introduce uninformative simplified phrases.

This study was based on, and tended to support Bernstein's (1961) hypothesis that the middle class can use an elaborated code of language as well as a restricted code. The working class however may only be able to use a restricted code, even where the situation seems to require elaborated information. Elaborated answers to children's questions open up possibilities for the child, provide accurate information and point to possible causal factors. Restricted answers to questions provide closed responses, over-simplified, and appealing to authority.

The implication of this research into language codes is that where only a restricted code is in use in the home there will be discontinuity with the school where the language of teaching is elaborated. Obviously the actual situation is more complicated than this. It is not clear whether Bernstein is discussing the working class as a whole or only the unskilled. In practice there is not likely to be a clear distinction between the middle class with access to both types of code and a working class with one only. The situation among the bulk of the population of skilled and white collar workers is likely to be very confused.

Bernstein and Henderson (1969) suggest that differences in the use of language in the home influence the opportunities for children to learn the basic skills and personal relations that serve as the foundation for school work. Knowledge in the working class homes seemed to be passed to the child in a situation in which he was expected to be passive. The middle class child was expected to explore problems himself, using information provided by the parents. The working class child learned the skills, but the middle class child was learning not only the skills but also the principles behind them. The middle class child is taught to help himself to learn. He is socialized through an elaborated code so that he can reflect upon his own position in social relationships. Obviously this combination of abilities provides an ideal preparation for schooling. He is prepared to learn actively and to adjust to new personal relations, particularly towards those in authority. The working class child is liable to be passive in the classroom and less able to handle novel personal relations. Family and school reinforce the socialization of the middle class child but there are discrepancies for the working class.

Bernstein and Brandis (1970), using a Maternal Index of Communication and Control, confirm this discontinuity for working class children in school and their consequent learning handicap. In this study the mothers in middle and working class groups were using language in radically differing ways as they explained things to their children, exercised control over them and responded to children's questions. The middle class mothers were expanding, opening up the children's world through a sensitivity to actions and words. The world of the working class child was being restricted and closed and their mothers were more likely to be responsive to words but not actions. The middle class child was influenced reciprocally by home and school. The working class child could be experiencing hostility between parents and teachers. Robinson and Rackstraw (1972) support this hypothesis from the evidence of their own observations of children's verbal behaviour.

Bernstein and Brandis express these relations between home and school with caution. The evidence comes from the mothers' answers to questions, not their actual behaviour. The terms middle and working class are very crude categories. Within each class there are wide differences in early experience. Scores on an Index have to be related to the complex interaction of many persons that makes up a family and a school. There is not yet evidence on the way children control the responses of parents. Examples of the complicated underworld of family life appear in Bernstein and Brandis. In middle class homes the crucial person seemed to be the mother and all children were benefiting by an elaboration of their speech and a favourable attitude towards schooling. In the working class family the crucial person was the child. If he was of high ability he received more stimulation and support than if he showed signs of being less able. Another example was that while working class mothers seemed to communicate with and control boys and girls in similar ways, in middle class families the mothers were more coercive with daughters and explained less to them than to their brothers. These findings may prove highly significant when followed up. What they indicate now is that differences can be detected, but their explanation often involves generalization and informed guesswork.

This work of the Sociological Research Unit provides a fitting conclusion to a study of socialization. It illustrates first how difficult it is to go beyond finding out that differences exist between social classes, to answer the question 'why do they occur?' The research reported in this book lies between two contrasting types. At one extreme there are investigations into natural situations in family and school. These may have provided valuable insights but there are too many factors in natural situations for the research to be completely reliable. At the other extreme there are experimental studies where all but a single factor have been controlled. Here the method may be reliable, but the results come from such a synthetic situation that generalization is impossible. Most of the evidence in this book lies somewhere between these extremes.

The alternative models presented by Byrne and Williamson (1972) under the title, 'The Myth of the Restricted Code', illustrate the impossibility of certainty. By using a 'resource provision' model rather than one based on different linguistic codes they could present data indicating that the restricted code model could only explain a very small residual in variation in attainment and was of very little practical significance for formulating policy. Their conclusions were that what was really needed was a redistribution of available resources, not fiddling about with educational priority areas and curriculum reform. Strangely, this is also the view of Bernstein whom they were criticising.

This use of the word 'myth' is a caution about the use of research evidence. Once the influence of various forms of deprivation in the social background of the child had been shown to be associated with under-achievement in school there was a tendency to assume that remedies had to be sought outside the classroom. At its worst this led to dismissing the possibility of an academic education for the working class because cultural deprivation was the paramount influence. This was never in the minds of the researchers, but was one possible interpretation. In reality the research had never been focused on the way learning situations in schools could be organized to benefit children from a variety of backgrounds. The evidence from research reflects the questions asked at the start by the researchers. Different questions, on the way schooling may contribute to good or poor performance, might have produced evidence showing the classroom experience as a potent force in determining not only achievement, but personality.

The relation of family and school in socialization is a particularly difficult field to investigate. We do not know which are the crucial factors. We can not tell how these factors interact in family or school or between them. When single factors are discussed their inter-relation with others is being ignored. The behaviour that is observed, questioned or measured may only be a symptom not a cause. It was easy to demonstrate that the context of family and school life has changed. It was easy to show that social class differences exist. But once the problem was to find out why these differences appear to be so important, the analysis has to go deeper and the methods of investigation may appear superficial.

The message that comes out of any study of home and school is that both are deeply involved in education and can only be artificially separated. This is why the possibility of discontinuity for some children is so unfortunate. But this finding has also to be seen as a problem of the nature of social scientific evidence. As the search for the reasons why deepens, it becomes increasingly difficult to uncover relevant evidence. Once explanations of differing attainment, perception and motivation are seen to lie in the distribution of values, in the differing construction of pictures of the world, in the way individuals and groups negotiate the meaning of events, social scientists have to use softer and softer evidence. The exposure of folklore as fiction, the challenging of accepted myths, the illumination of unjust, unequal and inefficient practices, the provision of information for new policies, and predictions about the effects of old ones and the accumulation of evidence about human behaviour are among the contributions of social science. But this body of knowledge is always under challenge, always changing. The consequent redundancy is a warning. Today's dogma is in tomorrow's dustbin.

List of references

Chapter One

AMMAR, H. (1954). *Growing up in an Egyptian Village*. London: Routledge & Kegan Paul

ANDERSON, M. (1971). 'Family, Household and the Industrial Revolution', in ANDERSON, M. (Ed.), *Sociology of the Family*. London: Penguin, pp. 78–98.

ARIES, P. (1962). *Centuries of Childhood*. London: Cape.

BANKS, J. A. (1954). *Prosperity and Parenthood*. London: Routledge & Kegan Paul.

BOAS, G. (1966). *The Cult of Childhood*. London: Warburg Institute.

BRONFENBRENNER, U. (1972). 'Another world of childhood', *New Society*. 19, 489, pp. 279–86.

COVENEY, P. (1957). *Poor Monkey*. London: Rockcliff.

JORDAN, W. K. (1959). *Philanthropy in England, 1480–1660*. London: Allen & Unwin.

EARLE, J. (1628). *Microcosmographie*. Quoted in BOAS *op. cit.* p. 42.

GULLIVER, P. H. (1963). *Social Control in an African Society*. London: Routledge & Kegan Paul.

KENYATTA, J. (1953). *Facing Mount Kenya*. London: Secker and Warburg.

LASLETT, P. (1965). *The World we have lost*. London: Methuen.

MANCHESTER STATISTICAL SOCIETY. (1834, 1835 & 1838). *Reports*. Manchester.

MEAD, M. (1964). *Sex and Temperament in Three Primitive Societies*. London: Routledge & Kegan Paul. (First published in 1935).

MOUMOUNI, A. (1968). *Education in Africa*. London: Deutsch.

MUSGROVE, F. (1966). *The Family, Education and Society*. London: Routledge & Kegan Paul.

PATON, X. and BELOFF, H. (1970). 'Bronfenbrenner's moral dilemma in Britain: Children, their peers and parents', *International Journal of Psychology*, 5, pp. 27–32.

PINCHBECK, I. and HEWITT, M. (1969). *Children in English Society, Vol. 1*. London: Routledge & Kegan Paul.

ROSSER, C. and HARRIS, C. C. (1965). *The Family and Social Change*. London: Routledge & Kegan Paul.

SANGSTER, P. (1963). *Pity my Simplicity*. London: Epworth.

SHIPMAN, M. D. (1971). *Education and Modernization*. London: Faber & Faber.

Silver, H. (1965). *The Concept of Popular Education*. London: McGibbon & Kee.

Smelser, N. (1959). *Social Change in the Industrial Revolution*. London: Routledge and Kegan Paul.

Smith, F. (1931). *History of English Elementary Education*. London: University of London Press.

Tanner, J. M. (1961). *Education and Physical Growth*. London: University of London Press.

Willmott, P. and Young, M. (1960). *Family and Class in a London Suburb*. London: Routledge & Kegan Paul.

Young, M. and Willmott, P. (1957). *Family and Kinship in East London*. London: Routledge & Kegan Paul.

Chapter Two

Barnett, A. (1961). *The Human Species*. London: Pelican.

Bronfenbrenner, U. (1972). 'Another World of Childhood', *New Society*, 10/2/1972, pp. 279–86.

Cannon, C. (1964). 'The Influence of Religion on Educational Policy, 1902–44'. *Brit. J. of Ed. Studies*, XII, 2, pp. 143–60.

Dearden, R. F. (1968). *The Philosophy of Primary Education*. London: Routledge & Kegan Paul.

Douglas, J. W. B. and Blomfield, J. M. (1958). *Children Under Five*. London: Allen & Unwin.

Jephcott, P., Seear, N. and Smith, J. H. (1962). *Married Women Working*. London: Allen & Unwin.

Inglis, K. S. (1960). 'Patterns of Worship in 1851', *J. Ecclesiastical History.*, pp. 74–86.

Klein, J. (1965). *Samples from English Cultures*. London: Routledge & Kegan Paul.

Liddiard, M. (1928). *The Mothercraft Manual*, 6th ed. London: Churchill.

Martin, D. (1967). *A Sociology of English Religion*. London: SCM.

Moore, T. W. (1967). 'The effects of substitute mothers', *New Society*, 10, 263, p. 522.

Myrdal, A. and Klein, V. (1956). *Women's Two Roles: Home and Work*. London: Routledge & Kegan Paul.

Peters, R. S. (Ed.) (1969). *Perspectives on Plowden*. London: Routledge & Kegan Paul.

Royal Commission on Population. (1949). *Report*. London: HMSO.

Royal Commission on Population. (1949). *Family Census*. London: HMSO.

Shipman, M. D. (1972). *The Limitations of Social Research*. London: Longmans.

Spock, B. (1945). *Baby and Child Care*. New York: Simon and Schuster.

Spock, B. (1962). *Problems of Parents*. London: Bodley Head.

Titmuss, R. M. (1963). *Essays on 'The Welfare State'*. London: Allen Univ. Books.

Taconis, L. (1969). 'The Role of the Contemporary Father in Rearing Young Children', *Educ. Res.*, 11, 2 83–94.

Watson, J. B. (1928). *Psychological Care of Infant and Child*. New York: W. W. Norton.

Wolfenstein, M. (1950–51). 'The Emergence of Fun Morality', *J. Soc. Issues*, 6/7, pp. 15–25.

Yudkin, S. and Holme, A. (1963). *Working Mothers and their Children*. London: M. Joseph.

Chapter Three

Barry, H., Bacon, M. K. and Child, I. L. (1957). 'A cross-cultural survey of some sex differences in socialization', *J. abn. Social Psychology*, 55, pp. 327–32.

Berger, P. L. and Luckmann, T. (1971). *The Social Construction of Reality*. London: Penguin.

Bernstein, B. (1971). 'On the Classification and Framing of Educational Knowledge', in Young, M. F. D. *Knowledge and Control*. London: Collier-Macmillan, pp. 47–69.

Finlayson, D. S. and Cohen, L. (1967). 'The teacher's role: a comparative study of the conceptions of College of Education students and Head teachers', *Brit. J. of Ed. Psychol.* 37, 1, pp. 22–31.

Goffman, E. (1968). *Asylums*. London: Penguin.

Hartup, W. W. and Zoo, K. E. A. (1960). 'Sex-role preference in 3- and 4-year-old children', *J. Consultive Psychol.* 24, pp. 420–26.

Haufmann, E. (1963). 'Social structure of a group of kindergarten children', in Charters, W. W. and Gage, N. L. *Readings in the Social Psychology of Education*. New York: Allyn and Bacon.

Hindley, C. B. (1965). 'Stability and change in abilities up to five years: group trends', *J. Child Psychol. and Psychiatry*, 6, pp. 85–100.

Hirst, P. H. (1965). 'Liberal education and the Nature of knowledge', in Archambault, R. D. (Ed.) *Philosophical Analysis of Education*, London: Routledge & Kegan Paul.

May, D. E. (1963). *Children in Nursery School*. London: Univ. of London Press.

Mead, G. H. (1934). *Mind, Self and Society*. Chicago: Univ. of Chicago Press.

Mead, M. (1964). *Sex and Temperament in Three Primitive Societies*. London: Routledge & Kegan Paul. (first published 1935).

Schaffer, H. R. (1971). *The growth of sociability*. London: Penguin.

Shipman, M. D. (1967). 'Theory and Practice in the Education of Teachers', *Educ. Res.*, 9, 3, pp. 208–12.

Shipman, M. D. (1971). 'Curriculum for inequality', in Hooper, R. (Ed.) *The Curriculum*. Edinburgh: Oliver and Boyd.

Spencer, W. B. and Gillen, F. J. (1927). *The Arunta*. London: Univ. of London Press.

White, J. (1968). 'Instruction in Obedience', *New Society*. 2/5/1968.

Young, M. F. D. (1971). 'An Approach to the Study of Curricula as Socially Organized Knowledge', in Young, M. F. D. (Ed.) *Knowledge and Control*. London: Collier-MacMillan, pp. 19–46.

Chapter Four

Ainsworth, M. D. (1962). *Deprivation of Maternal Care and Reassessment of its Effects*. Geneva: WHO.

Andry, R. C. (1960). *Delinquency and Paternal Pathology*. London: Methuen.

Bernstein, B. and Young, D. (1967). 'Social Class Differences in Conceptions of the Use of Toys', *Sociology*, 1, pp. 131–40.

Blood, R. O. and Wolfe, D. M. (1960). *Husbands and Wives: the Dynamics of Married Living*. New York: Free Press.

Bossard, H. S. and Boll, E. S. (1950). *Ritual in Family Living*. Philadelphia: University of Pennsylvania Press.

Bossard, H. S. and Boll, E. S. (1966). *The Sociology of Child Development*. New York: Harper and Row.

Bowlby, J. (1951). *Maternal Care and Mental Health*. Geneva: W.H.O.

Chapman, D. (1955). *The Home and Social Status*. London: Routledge & Kegan Paul.

Cowie, J., Cowie, V. and Slater, E. (1968). *Delinquency in Girls*. London: Heinemann.

Dennis, N., Henriques, F. M. and Slaughter, C. (1957). *Coal is our Life*. London: Eyre and Spottiswoode.

Durkheim, E. (1912). Les formes élémentaires de la vie réligieuse. Paris: Librarie Felix Alcan.

Fletcher, R. (1962). *The Family and Marriage*. London: Penguin.

Gibson, H. B. and West, D. J. (1968). *Some Concomitants of Early Delinquency*. Cambridge: Institute of Criminology. (in draft). Reported in Holman, R. (Ed.), *Socially Deprived Families*. London: Bedford Square Press, 1970.

Goldthorpe, J. H., *et al. The Affluent Worker and the Class Structure*. Cambridge: Cambridge Univ. Press.

Jones, J. (1966). 'Social Class and the under-fives', *New Society*, 221, pp. 935–6.

King, F. T. (1937). *Feeding and Care of Baby*. Oxford: Oxford Univ. Press.

Kysar, J. E. (1968). 'Reactions of professionals to disturbed children and their parents', *Archives of General Psychiatry*, 19, pp. 562–70.

Landis, J. T. and Landis, M. G. (1963). *Building a Successful Marriage*. Englewood Cliffs: Prentice-Hall.

Leach, E. (1967). 'Ourselves and Others', *Listener*, 30 Nov.

MOGEY, J. M. (1956). *Family and Neighbourhood*. Oxford: Oxford Univ. Press.

NEWSON, J. and NEWSON, E. (1963). *Infant Care in an Urban Community*. London: Allen & Unwin.

NEWSON, J. and NEWSON, E. (1968). *Four Years Old in an Urban Community*. London: Allen & Unwin.

PARSONS, T. (1955). 'The American family: its relations to personality and the social structure', in PARSONS, T. and BALES, R. F., *Family Socialization and Interaction Process*, New York: Free Press, pp. 3–21.

REGISTRAR-GENERAL, (1968). *Statistical Review*. London: HMSO.

RHEINGOLD, H. L. (1969). 'The Social and Socializing Infant', in GOSLIN, D. A., *Handbook of Socialization Theory and Research*. Chicago: Rand, McNally, pp. 779–87.

CENTRAL STATISTICAL OEFICE, (1970). *Social Trends*. London: HMSO.

WALTERS, J. and STINNETT, N. (1971). 'Parent-Child Relationships: A Decade Review of Research', *J. Marriage and the Family*, 33, 1, pp. 70–111.

WILLMOTT, P. and YOUNG, M. (1960). *Family and Class in a London Suburb*. London: Routledge & Kegan Paul.

WILSON, H. (1962). *Delinquency and Child Neglect*. London: Allen & Unwin.

WOOTTON, B. (1959). *Social Science and Social Pathology*. London: Allen & Unwin.

YOUNG, M. and WILLMOTT, P. (1957). *Family and Kinship in East London*. London: Routledge & Kegan Paul.

Chapter Five

ALLEN, E. A. (1961). 'Attitudes to school and teachers in a secondary modern school', *Brit. J. Ed. Psychol.*, 31, pp. 106–9.

AMIDON, E. and HOUGH, J. (1967). *Interaction Analysis*. New York: Addison Wesley.

ANDERSON, H. H. and BREWER, H. M. (1945, 1946). 'Studies of teachers' classroom personalities', *Applied Psychology Monographs*, Stanford: Stanford Univ. Press.

ANDERSON, R. C. (1963). 'Learning in discussion: a resume of the authoritarian-democratic studies', in CHARTERS, W. W. and GAGE, N. L., *Readings in the Social Psychology of Education*. New York: Allyn & Bacon, pp. 153–62.

BARKER LUNN, J. C. (1970). *Streaming in the Primary School*, Slough: NFER.

BARKER LUNN, J. C. (1971). *Social Class, Attitudes and Achievements*, Slough: NFER.

BARNES, D. (1971). 'Classroom Contexts for Language and Learning'. *Educ. Rev.*, 23, 3, pp. 235–48.

BARNES, D., BRITTON, J. and ROSEN, H. (1969). *Language, the Learner and the School*. London: Penguin.

BERNSTEIN, B., ELVIN, H. L. and PETERS, R. S. (1966). 'Ritual in Education', *Philosophical Transactions of the Royal Society of London*, pp. 429–36.

BYRNE, D. (1961). 'The influence of propinquity and opportunities for interaction on classroom relationships', *Human Relations*, 14, pp. 63–9.

CLAIBORN, W. L. (1969). 'Expectancy Effects in the Classroom: A Failure to Replicate', *J. Ed. Psychol.* 69, pp. 377–83.

COHEN, L. C. and COHEN, A. C. (1970). 'A Tribute of Success in Primary School', *Durham Res. Rev.*, 5, 24, pp. 449–54.

DANIELS, J. C. (1961). 'The Effects of Streaming in the Primary School', *Brit. J. Ed. Psychol.*, 1, pp. 69–78.

DOUGLAS, J. W. B. (1964). *The Home and the School*. London: MacGibbon & Kee.

GABRIEL, J. G. (1957). *An Analysis of the Emotional Problems of the Teacher in the Classroom*. Melbourne: F. W. Cheshire.

GEER, B. (1971). 'Teaching', in School and Society Course Team (Eds.), *School and Society*, London: Routledge & Kegan Paul, pp. 3–8.

HALLWORTH, H. J. (1962). 'A teacher's perception of his pupils', *Ed. Rev.*, 14, pp. 124–33.

HARGREAVES, D. H. (1967). *Social Relations in a Secondary School*. London: Routledge & Kegan Paul.

HOLT, J. (1969). *How Children Fail*. New York: Pitman.

JACKSON, P. W. and BELFORD, E. (1965). 'Educational Objectives and the Joys of Teaching', *School Review*, Autumn, pp. 267–91.

JACKSON, P. W. and BELFORD, E. (1967). 'Private Affairs in Public Settings: Observations on Teaching in Elementary Schools', *School Review*, Summer, pp. 172–86.

LACEY, C. (1970). *Hightown Grammar*. Manchester: Manchester U. Press.

LEWIN, K., LIPPITT, R. and WHITE, R. K. (1967). 'Patterns of Aggressive Behaviour in Experimentally Created "Social Climates"', in AMIDON, E. and HOUGH, J., *Interaction Analysis*, New York: Addison Wesley.

LIPPITT, R. and WHITE, R. K. (1965). 'An Experimental Study of Leadership and Group Life', in PROSHANSKY, H. P. and SEIDENBERG, B., *Basic Studies in Social Psychology*. New York: Holt, Rinehart and Winston, pp. 523–37.

MCINTYRE, D., MORRISON, A. and SUTHERLAND, J. (1966). 'Social and educational variables relating to teachers' assessments of primary school pupils', *Brit. J. Ed. Psychol.*, 36, pp. 272–9.

NASH, R. (1971). 'Camouflage in the Classroom', *New Society*, 18, 447, pp. 667–9.

PIDGEON, D. A. (1970). *Expectation and Pupil Performance*. Slough: NFER.

PRECKER, J. A. (1952). 'Similarity of valuings as a factor in selection of peers and near-authority figures', *J. Abnormal and Soc. Psychol.*, 47, pp. 406–14.

ROSENTHAL, R. (1966). *Experimenter Effects in Behavioural Research.* New York: Appleton-Century-Crofts.

ROSENTHAL, R. and JACOBSON, L. (1968). *Pygmalion in the Classroom.* New York: Holt, Rinehart and Winston.

RUBINSTEIN, D. (1969). *School Attendance in London,* 1870–1904: *A Social History.* Hull: Univ. of Hull Occasional Papers in Economics and Social History.

SCHOOLS COUNCIL, (1968). *Enquiry 1: Young School Leavers.* London: HMSO.

SEABORNE, M. (1971). *Primary School Design.* London: Routledge & Kegan Paul.

SHIPMAN, M. D. (1971). 'Innovation in Schools', in WALTON, J. (Ed.). *Curriculum Organization and Design.* London: Ward Lock, pp. 11–16.

STAINES, J. W. (1958). 'The Self-picture as a factor in the classroom', *B. J. Ed. Psychol.,* 28, 97–111.

SUGARMAN, B. (1970). 'Classroom friends and leaders', *New Society,* 15, (382) pp. 141–2.

TAYLOR, P. H. (1962). 'Children's evaluations of the chacteristics of the good teacher', *Brit. J. Ed. Psych.,* 32, pp. 258–66.

TAYLOR, P. H. (1968). 'Teachers' Role conflicts—11. English Infant and Junior Schools', *Int. J. Ed. Science,* 2, pp. 167–73.

TAYLOR, P. H. (1970). *How Teachers Plan their courses.* Slough: NFER.

THORNDIKE, R. L. (1968). 'Review of Rosenthal and Jacobson's Pygmalion in the Classroom', *Am. Ed. Res. Assn.,* 4, pp. 708–11. See also SNOW, R., 'Review of Rosenthal and Jacobson's Pygmalion in the Classroom', *Contemporary Psychology,* 14, pp. 197–9.

WERTHMAN, C. (1971). 'Delinquents in Schools', in School and Society course team (Eds.), *School and Society,* London: Routledge & Kegan Paul, pp. 39–48.

WHITE, R. K. and LIPPITT, R. L. (1960). *Autocracy and Democracy.* New York: Harper.

WICKMAN, E. K. (1928). *Children's Behaviour and Teacher's Attitudes.* New York: Commonwealth Fund.

WILLIG, C. J. (1963). 'Social implications of streaming in a junior school', *Educ. Res.,* 5, 2, pp. 151–4.

WOLFSON, B. J. and JACKSON, P. W. (1968). 'Varieties of constraint in a nursery school', *Young Children,* 23, pp. 358–67.

Chapter Six

BERNSTEIN, B. (1970). 'Education cannot compensate for society', *New Society,* 15 (387), pp. 344–7.

CENTRAL ADVISORY COUNCIL FOR EDUCATION (1967). *Children and their Primary Schools.* (Plowden Report). London: HMSO.

CENTRAL STATISTICAL OFFICE (1970). *Social Trends.* London: HMSO.

CHAZAN, M., LAING, A. and JACKSON, S. (1971). *Just Before School.* Oxford: Blackwell.

DEPARTMENT OF EMPLOYMENT AND PRODUCTIVITY. (1967). *Family Expenditure Survey.* London: HMSO.

DOUGLAS, J. W. B. and ROSS, J. M. (1964). 'Subsequent Progress of Nursery School Children', *Educ. Res.*, 7, pp. 83–94.

DOUGLAS, J. W. B., ROSS, J. M. and SIMPSON, H. R. (1968). *All our Future.* London: Peter Davies.

DREEBEN, R. (1968). *On What is Learned in School.* New York: Addison Wesley.

FLOUD, J., HALSEY, A. H. and MARTIN, F. M. (1956). *Social Class and Educational Opportunity.* London: Heinemann.

FRASER, E. (1959). *Home Environment and the School.* London: London Univ. Press.

GOODACRE, E. J. (1968). *Teachers and their Pupils' Home Background.* Slough: NFER.

HOLT, J. (1969). *How Children Fail.* New York: Pitman.

ILLICH, I. (1971). *De-schooling Society.* London: Calder & Boyars.

JACKSON, D. and MARSDEN, D. (1962). *Education and the Working Class.* London: Routledge & Kegan Paul.

JACKSON, P. W. (1968). *Life in Classrooms.* New York: Holt, Rinehart and Winston.

JONES, J. (1966). 'Social Class and the under-fives', *New Society*, 221, pp. 935–6.

MARTIN, F. M. (1954). 'An Inquiry into Parents' preferences in Secondary Education', in GLASS, D. V. (Ed.) *Social Mobility.* London: Routledge & Kegan Paul, pp. 51–75.

MIDWINTER, E. (1970). 'Curriculum and the EPA community school'. HOOPER, R. (Ed.), *The Curriculum.* Edinburgh: Oliver and Boyd, pp. 483–98.

MOORE, T. W. (1966). 'The trouble with school', Univ. of London, *Inst. of Ed. Bull.*, 9, pp. 19–21.

NISBET, J. D. (1953). *Family Environment: A Direct Effect of Family Size on Intelligence.* London: Eugenics Society.

PALMER, R. (1971). *Starting School.* London: Univ. of London Press.

PEAKER, G. F. (1971). *Starting School.* London: Univ. London Press.

PEAKER, G. F. (1971). *The Plowden Children Four Years Later.* Slough: NFER.

ROSSER, C. and HARRIS, C. C. (1965). *The Family and Social Change.* London: Routledge & Kegan Paul.

SMELSER, N. (1959). *Social Change in the Industrial Revolution.* London: Routledge & Kegan Paul.

TENNANT, T. G. (1971). 'School Non-Attendance and Delinquency', *Educ. Res.*, 13, 3, pp. 185–97.

Wolfson, B. J. and Jackson, P. W. (1969). 'An Intensive Look at the Daily Experiences of Young Children', *Research into Education*, 2, pp. 1–12.

Chapter Seven

Abel-Smith, B. and Townsend, P. (1965). *The Poor and the Poorest*. London: G. Bell.
Booth, C. (1902). *Life and Labour of the Prople in London*. London: Macmillan.
Byrne, D. S. and Williamson, W. (1972). 'Some intra-regional variations in educational provision and their bearing upon educational attainment —the case of the North East', *Sociology*, 6, 1, pp. 71–87.
Central Advisory Council for Education (1967). *Children and their Primary Schools*, (Plowden Report). London: HMSO.
Central Statistical Office. *Social Trends*. London: HMSO.
Crawford, M. D., Gardner, M. J. and Morris, J. N. (1968). 'Mortality and Hardness of Local Water-supplies', *Lancet*, 1, pp. 827–39 and p. 1092.
Crellin, E., Kellmer Pringle, M. L. and West, P. (1971). *Born Illegitimate*. Slough: NFER.
Cullingworth, J. B. (1965). *Scottish Housing in* 1965. Glasgow: Scottish Development Department.
Department of Employment and Productivity. (1967). *Gazette*, May. London: HMSO.
Douglas, J. W. B. and Blomfield, J. M. (1958). *Children under five*. London: Allen & Unwin.
Harvey, A. (1969). 'Homeless? You can't come here', *New Society*, 13, 335 pp. 323–4.
Holman, R. (1972). *Unsupported Mothers and the Care of their Children*. London: Mothers in Action.
Jephcott, P. (1971). *Homes in High Flats*. Edinburgh: Oliver & Boyd.
Lambert, R. (1964). *Nutrition in Britain*, 1950–1960. London: Codicote Press.
Maizels, J. (1961). *Two to five in high flats*. London: The Housing Centre.
Marsden, D. (1968). *Mothers Alone*. London: Allen Lane.
Ministry of Housing. (1968). *House Conditions Survey*. London: HMSO.
Ministry of Social Security. (1967). *Circumstances of Families*. London: HMSO.
Ministry of Social Security. (1967). *Administration of the Wage Stop*. London: HMSO.
Packman, M. and Power, J. (1968). 'Children in need and the help they receive', in *Report of the Committee on Local Authority and Allied Personal Social Services* (Seebowm report), London: HMSO, Appendix Q, pp. 347–56.
Philp, A. F. (1964). *Family Failure*. London: Faber & Faber.

Pond, D. A. and Arie, T. (1971). 'Services for Children in Trouble', *Child Care*, 25, 1, pp. 16–20.

Registrar-General. (1967). *Statistical Review of England and Wales*. London: HMSO.

Rowntree, B. S. (1901). *Poverty*. London: Nelson.

Rowntree, B. S. and Lavers, G. R. (1951). *Poverty and the Welfare State*. London: Longmans.

Rutter, M., Tizard, J. and Whitmore, K. (1970). *Education, Health and Behaviour*. London: Longmans.

Taylor, G. and Ayres, N. (1969). *Born and Bred Unequal*. London: Longmans.

Westergaard, J. and Little, A. (1970). 'Educational Opportunity and social selection in England and Wales: trends and policy implications', in Craft, M. (Ed.) *Family, Class and Education*. London: Longmans, pp. 49–71.

Wimperis, V. (1960). *The Unmarried Mother and her Child*. London: Allen & Unwin.

Woolf, M. (1967). *The Housing Survey in England and Wales*. London: Government Social Survey.

Wynn, M. (1964). *Fatherless Families*. London: M. Joseph.

Chapter Eight

Armstrong, M. (1969). 'Reorganization is not enough', *Times Ed. Supp.*, 5/12/1969, p. 4.

Barnes, D., Britton, J. and Rosen, H. (1969). *Language, the Learner and the School*. London: Penguin.

Barnes, D. (1971). 'Language and Learning in the Classroom'. *J. Curric. Studies*, 3, 1, pp. 27–38.

Benn, C. and Simon, B. (1970). *Half way there*. London: McGraw-Hill.

Bernstein, B. (1961). 'Social Class and Linguistic Development'. in Halsey, A. H., Floud, J. and Anderson, C. A., *Education, Economy and Society*. New York: Free Press.

Bernstein, B. (1970). 'A Critique of the Concept of "Compensatory Education" ', in Rubenstein, D. and Stoneman, C. (Eds.) *Education for Democracy*, London: Penguin, pp. 110–21.

Central Advisory Council for Education (1954). *Early Leaving*. London: HMSO.

Central Advisory Council for Education (1959). 15 *to* 18 (Crowther Report). London: HMSO.

Central Advisory Council for Education (1967). *Children and their Primary Schools* (Plowden Report). London: HMSO.

Committee on Higher Education. (1963). *Higher Education* (Robbins Report). London: HMSO.

Daniels, J. C. (1959). 'Some effects of segregation and streaming on the intellectual and scholastic development of Junior School children', Ph.D. thesis, Univ. Nottingham.

DAVIE, R., BUTLER, N. and GOLDSTEIN, H. (1972). *From Birth to Seven.* London: Longmans.

DOUGLAS, J. W. B. (1964). *The Home and the School.* London: MacGibbon & Kee.

DOUGLAS, J. W. B. and BLOMFIELD, J. M. (1958). *Children under five.* London: Allen & Unwin.

DOUGLAS, J. W. B. and ROSS, J. M. (1965). 'The effects of absence on primary school performance', *Brit. J. Ed. Psychol.*, 35, 1. pp. 28–40.

FISHER, D. G. (1972). 'Streaming and Social Class in the Comprehensive School', M. Sc. Thesis, Univ. Bradford.

FORD, J. (1969). *Social Class and the Comprehensive School.* London: Routledge & Kegan Paul.

FLOUD, J. and HALSEY, A. H. (1957). 'Intelligence Tests and Selection for Secondary Schools', *Brit. J. Soc.*, 8, 1, pp. 33–9.

FLOUD, J., HALSEY, A. H. and MARTIN, F. M. (1956). *Social Class and Educational Opportunity.* London: Heinemann.

FRASER, E. (1959). *Home Environment and the School.* London: Univ. London Press.

GRAY, J. L. and MOSHINSKY, P. (1938). in HOGBEN, L. (Ed.), *Political Arithmetic.* London: Allen & Unwin.

HARGREAVES, D. H. (1967). *Social Relations in a Secondary School.* London: Routledge & Kegan Paul.

HINDLEY, C. B. (1965). 'Stability and Change in Abilities up to five years: group trends', *J. Child Psychol and Psychiatry* 6, pp. 85–100.

HOLLY, D. N. (1965). 'Profiting from a Comprehensive School: Class, Sex and Ability', *Brit. J. Soc.*, 16, 4, 150–8.

JACKSON, B. and MARSDEN, D. (1962). *Education and the Working Class.* London: Routledge & Kegan Paul.

KELLMER PRINGLE, M. L., BUTLER, M. L. and DAVIE, R. (1966). 11,000 *seven year olds.* London: Longmans.

KLEIN, J. (1965). *Samples from English Cultures.* London: Routledge & Kegan Paul.

LACEY, C. (1970). *Hightown Grammar.* Manchester: Univ. Manchester Press.

LINDSAY, K. (1926). *Social Progress and Educational Waste.* London: Routledge.

LUNN, J. C. B. (1970). *Streaming in the Primary School.* Slough: NFER.

MOORE, T. (1967). 'Language and Intelligence, Part 1', *Human Development*, II, pp. 1–24.

MORRIS, J. M. (1966). *Standards and Progress in Reading.* Slough: NFER.

NEWSON, J. and NEWSON, E. (1963). *Infant Care in an Urban Community.* London: Allen & Unwin.

NEWSON, J. and NEWSON, E. (1968). *Four Years Old in an Urban Community.* London: Allen & Unwin.

SAMPSON, O. C. (1956). 'A Study of speech development in children of 18–30 months', *Brit. J. Educ. Psychol.*, 26, 194–201.

SHIPMAN, M. D. (1972). *The Limitations of Social Research*. London: Longmans.

SPINLEY, B. (1954). *The Deprived and the Privileged*. London: Routledge & Kegan Paul.

SURREY EDUCATIONAL RESEARCH ASSOCIATION. (1968). *To Stream or not to Stream*.

TAPPER, T. (1971). *Young People and Society*. London: Faber & Faber.

WESTERGAARD, J. and LITTLE, A. (1967). 'Educational opportunity and social selection in England and Wales: trends and policy implications', in CRAFT, M. (Ed.), *Family, Class and Education*. London: Longmans, pp. 49–71.

WITKIN, R. W. (1971). 'Social Class Influence on the Amount and Type of Positive Evaluation of School Lessons', *Sociology*, 5, 2, 191–208.

YATES, A. and PIDGEON, D. A. (1959). 'The effects of streaming', *Educ. Res.*, 11, 1, 65–9.

YOUNG, M. F. D. (1971). *Knowledge and Control*. London: Collier-Macmillan.

Chapter Nine

ARGYLE, A. and ROBINSON, J. (1962). 'Two Origins of Achievement Motivation', *Brit. J. Soc. and Clin. Psychol.* 10, 3, pp. 107–20.

BERNSTEIN, B. (1961). 'Social Class and Linguistic Development: A Theory of Social Learning', in HALSEY, A. H., FLOUD, J. and ANDERSON, C. A., *Education, Economy and Society*, New York, Free Press, pp. 288–314.

BERNSTEIN, B. (1971). *Class Codes and Control*. London: Routledge & Kegan Paul.

BERNSTEIN, B. and BRANDIS, W. (1970). 'Social Class Differences in Communication and Control', in BRANDIS, W. and HENDERSON, D., *Social Class, Language and Communciation*. London: Routledge & Kegan Paul, pp. 93–129.

BERNSTEIN, B. and HENDERSON, D. (1969). 'Social class differences in the relevance of language to socialization', *Sociology*, 3, 1, pp. 1–20.

BLOOM, B. (1964). *Stability and Change in Human Characteristics*. New York: Wiley.

BRADBURN, N. M. and BERLEW, D. E. (1961). 'Need for Achievement motivation and English Industrial Growth', *Econ. Dev, and Cult. Change*, 10, 1, pp. 8–20.

BRUCKMANN, I. R. (1966). 'The relationship between achievement motivation and sex, social class, school stream and intelligence', *Brit. J. Soc. and Clin. Psychol*, 5, 211–20.

BYRNE, D. S. and WILLIAMSON, W. (1971). 'The Myth of the Restricted Code', *Working Papers in Sociology*, Dept. Sociology and Social Admin., Univ. Durham.

CENTRAL ADVISORY COUNCIL FOR EDUCATION (1967). *Children and their Primary Schools* (Plowden Report). London: HMSO.

CHAZAN, M., LAING, A. and JACKSON, S. (1971). *Just before School.* Oxford: Blackwell.

DOUGLAS, J. W. B. (1964). *The Home and the School.* London: MacGibbon & Kee.

EIDUSEN, B. T. (1962). *Scientists: their Psychological World.* New York: Basic Books.

EYSENCK, H. J. (1971). *Race, Intelligence and Education.* London: M. Temple Smith.

FRASER, E. (1959). *Home Environment and the School.* London: Univ. London Press.

GOLDTHORPE, J. H., *et al.* (1969). *The Affluent Worker in the Class Structure.* Cambridge: Cambridge Univ. Press.

HARTLEY, J., HOLT, J. and HOGARTH, F. W. (1971). 'Academic Motivation and Programmed Learning', *Brit. J. Ed. Psychol.*, 41, 2, pp. 171–83.

HEBB, D. O. (1949). *The Organization of Behaviour.* New York: Wiley.

HECKHAUSEN, H. (1967). *The Anatomy of Achievement Motivation.* New York: Academic Press.

HESS, R. D. and SHIPMAN, V. C. (1968). 'Maternal Influences upon Early Learning', in BEAR, R. M. (Ed.), *Early Education.* Chicago: Aldine Press, 91–103.

JACKSON, B. and MARSDEN, D. (1961). *Education and the Working Class.* London: Routledge & Kegan Paul.

JENSEN, A. R. (1971). 'How much can we boost IQ and scholastic achievement?', *Harvard Ed. Rev.*, Winter, pp. 1–123.

JONES, J. (1966). 'Social Class and the under-fives', *New Society*, 221, pp. 935–6.

KOHN, M. L. (1959). 'Social class and the Exercise of Parental Authority', *Am. Soc. Rev.*, 24, pp. 252–366.

LAVIN, D. E. (1965). *The Prediction of Academic Performance.* New York: Wiley.

LUNN, J. C. B. (1972). 'The influence of Sex, Achievement Level and Social Class on Junior School Children's Attitudes', *Brit. J. Ed. Psychol*, 41, 1, pp. 70–4.

LUPTON, T. and MITCHELL, D. (1954). *Neighbourhood and Community*, Liverpool: Liverpool Univ. Press.

McCLELLAND, D. C. (1953). *The Achievement Motive.* New York: Appleton-Century-Crofts.

McCLELLAND, D. C. (1958). 'Methods of measuring human motivation', in ATKINSON, J. W. (Ed.) *Motives in Fantasy, Action and Society.* New York: Van Nostrand.

MERTON, R. K. (1938). 'Science, Technology and Society in Seventeenth Century England', *Osiris*, 4, pp. 360–597. (Bruges: St. Catherine's Press.)

MILLER, G. W. (1971). *Educational Opportunity and the Home.* London: Longmans.

MUSGROVE, F. (1966). *The Family, Education and Society.* London: Routledge & Kegan Paul.

NISBET, J. O. (1953). 'Family Environment: A Direct Effect of Family Size on Environment', *Occasional Papers on Eugenics*, 8, London: Eugenics Society.

ROBINSON, W. P. and RACKSTRAW, S. J. (1967). 'Variations in Mothers' Answers to Children's Questions as a Function of Social Class, Verbal Intelligence Scores and Sex', *Sociology*, 1, 3, pp. 259–76.

ROBINSON, W. P. and RACKSTRAW, S. J. (1972). *A Question of Answers*. London: Routledge & Kegan Paul.

SHIPMAN, M. D. (1972). *The Limitations of Social Research*. London: Longmans.

STACEY, M. (1960). *Tradition and Change: A Study of Banbury*. Oxford: Oxford Univ. Press.

STRODBECK, F. L. (1962). 'Family Integration, Values and Achievement', in HALSEY, A. H., FLOUD, J. and ANDERSON, C. A., *Education, Economy and Society*, New York: Free Press, pp. 315–47.

SWIFT, D. F. (1966). 'Social class and achievement motivation', *Educ. Res.*, 8, 2, 83–95.

SWIFT, D. F. (1968). 'Social class and educational adaption', in BUTCHER, H. J., (Ed.), *Educational Research in Britain*. London: Univ. London Press.

VERNON, P. E. (1969). *Intelligence and Cultural Environment*. London: Methuen.

WARNER, W. L. and ABEGGLEN, J. A. (1955). *Big Business Leaders in America*. New York: Harper & Bros.

WEBER, M. (1931). *The Protestant Ethic and the Spirit of Capitalism*. London: Allen & Unwin.